triathlon
START TO FINISH

triathlon
START TO FINISH

SAM MURPHY

FIREFLY BOOKS

A FIREFLY BOOK

Published by Firefly Books Ltd. 2009

Cover design: Heidi Baker
Cover photographs: front top to bottom I-stock/Steve Lovegrove; Whole Picture Productions; Alamy/Robert Michael; back Whole Picture Productions; author photograph Jorn Tomter

First printing

Publisher Cataloging-in-Publication Data (U.S.)

Murphy, Sam.
    Triathlon : start to finish / Sam Murphy.
[176] p. : ill., col. photos. ; cm.
Includes index.
Summary: Includes aspects of training and racing for fun and fulfillment.
ISBN-13: 978-1-55407-497-6
ISBN-10: 1-55407-497-5
1. Triathlon -- Training.   2. Triathlon -- Psychological aspects.
I. Title.
796.42/57 dc22   GV1060.73.M877   2009

Library and Archives Canada Cataloguing in Publication

Murphy, Sam
    Triathlon : start to finish / Sam Murphy.
Includes index.
ISBN-13: 978-1-55407-497-6
ISBN-10: 1-55407-497-5
    1. Triathlon. 2. Triathlon--Training. I. Title.
GV1060.73.M87 2009   796.42'57   C2009-901048-8

Published in the United States by
Firefly Books (U.S.) Inc.
P.O. Box 1338, Ellicott Station
Buffalo, New York 14205

Published in Canada by
Firefly Books Ltd.
66 Leek Crescent
Richmond Hill, Ontario L4B 1H1

Acknowledgments

There are a number of people to whom I owe my heartfelt thanks for helping me turn this idea into reality. Richard Allen, for creating the training programs and tips, as well as sharing with me his expertise, experience, and good humor! Dan Bullock from SwimforTri, for the huge amount of work he put into the swimming section, Phil Cavell from CycleFit, for his great feedback on the cycling chapter, and physiotherapist Alan Watson from the Bimal Clinic for his valuable contributions on running. I'm also grateful to dietician Karen Reid for helping to shape the nutritional advice and to East London Triathletes club coach Dawn Hunter for her words of wisdom on many aspects of the text.

Thanks also to Andy Cook, Ryan Bowd, Mike Trees, and Helen Gorman for their contributions and to Caroline Taggart for being such an unflappable editor.

The photographs were shot mainly at Club la Santa in Lanzarote and at London Fields Lido by Vince Jones of Whole Picture Productions and Eddie Jacob respectively. Thanks to all the models — James Stewart, Daniel Shipton, Julie Eyles, Daniel Bullock, Eleanor Baker, and various attendees of the Neilson Adidas Eyewear Triathlon Camp in Greece — my favorite training venue!

Printed in Singapore by Tien-Wah Press

CONTENTS

INTRODUCTION

It's no surprise that more and more people are catching the triathlon bug. It's a fun, sociable sport, offering a tough but achievable challenge — not to mention getting you super fit. Figures show that triathlon is currently one of the fastest growing sports in the US. As an example, USA Triathlon, the ruling body for the sport, say that they have seen a 23 percent growth per year in triathlon participation from 2000-2006. An estimated 690,000 train for run/bike/swim events every year and registration for the 2008 Nation's Triathlon® To Benefit The Leukemia & Lymphoma Society has more than tripled in the past three years. More than 40 percent of those registered are women and, nationwide, women are helping to fuel the tremendous growth of this sport, both at the Olympic and amateur level.

For years, I had let triathlon pass me by. I was an avid runner who occasionally took to the pool or jumped on a bike to get from A to B, but triathlon? It looked far too complicated, competitive, and serious. And all that equipment, too! No thanks, I thought, I'll stick to my running shoes. But in 2006 I took up the offer of a media place in the London event, with a view to writing an article about it. I booked myself onto a training camp (more of those later) three months before the big day, and my triathlon learning curve began. By the end of the week-long camp, I was utterly hooked. If you like a physical challenge, I suspect you will be too, once you give it a go.

The unique thing about triathlon is that it is a continuous race against time, from start to finish. There's no stopping the clock while you struggle out of your wetsuit, take a sip of your isotonic drink, fix a puncture or lace up your running shoes! Transition — the switch from one sport to the next — is as much a part of the race as the swimming, biking, and running. Another distinctive feature is the age group structure, which ensures that you are competing against people within the same five-year age bracket as yourself, rather than having to pit yourself against athletes half your age.

Triathlons as we know them were hatched in San Diego back in 1974. It was another four years before the first Ironman — the ultimate triathlon challenge — was held in Kona, Hawaii, the venue that continues to host the annual Ironman World Championships. Over the next two decades, triathlon maintained its macho image and niche appeal — certainly not a sport for ordinary mortals to get involved in — but since its Olympic debut in Sydney in 2000, its popularity has burgeoned. Just like the marathon, triathlon is becoming an event that everyone wants to do "just once" — though few stick to the once-only pledge!

But unlike marathon running, a whole range of people can be good at triathlon. Not only does each discipline demand a different

configuration of fitness and technique, there are three — or, arguably, four — distinct opportunities to excel. A 6-foot-tall powerhouse may fly on the bike but suffer on the run, while a little excess body fat won't hold back a swimmer with superb technique . . . and anyone with dexterity and a quick mind can be a master of transition. While it's not exactly a level playing field, this certainly evens things out a bit and makes the sport incredibly exciting.

Not everyone who does a triathlon cares about the time on the finish clock, but most who take on the multisport challenge want to give it their best shot. It can be an intimidating prospect for the uninitiated. For a start, how on earth do you fit in training for three sports? How can you remain injury free while you do so? Should you focus on your strongest discipline or your weakest?

And then there's the race itself. Whether it's an Olympic distance event or the euphemistically named sprint (see Chapter One for more on race distances), you'll find your reserves of endurance, strength, and skill amply called upon — not to mention your mental resources. Not only do you have the formidable task of swimming, cycling, and running in quick succession — but also the practicalities of getting out of the water and onto a bike against the clock, of cycling in close proximity to others, and staying fueled up throughout the race. All of this takes practice, of course, but it's good to learn from other people's mistakes — and, hopefully, you will learn from some of mine! However, this isn't just a personal perspective on completing a successful triathlon — I've consulted sport scientists, coaches, and, of course, triathletes, to get the most up-to-date, useful, and practical information and advice to make sure your first race experiences are memorable for all the right reasons. Richard Allen, nine-time British Elite Champion and a former member of the Olympic team, now specializes in coaching and mentoring beginners, which is why he was the perfect person to devise the training programs for this book. You'll also find his "Voice of Experience" tips and insights in every chapter.

But before you read on, a word of warning. If you're looking for a book that will help you periodize your year into macro- and mesocycles, suggest how to fit in multiple training sessions in a day, or discuss which tires to buy to shave 0.001g off your bike's weight, you've come to the wrong place. Just because you want to do a triathlon or two — or two dozen, even — it doesn't mean you have to adopt the lifestyle of a professional triathlete. In my view, that assumption is just as outdated as the image of triathlon as a sport only for the super-fit hard-core. The ever-growing number of newbies taking up the sport stand testament to that — and like them, I believe the best reason of all for doing triathlon is that it's fun!

Whether your goal is simply to get around your chosen race in one piece or break 2 hours 20 for the Olympic distance — I hope that *Triathlon: Start to Finish* will help you on your way.

CHAPTER ONE **THE START LINE**

So you're ready to take on the triathlon challenge. Well, you'll be pleased to hear that, contrary to popular myth, it won't entail seven days a week of grueling training, or shaving off your body hair, or remortgaging the house in order to buy a hi-tech bike. Of course, it will take you longer to make progress if you can only devote three hours per week to training rather than six or seven — but you will still get there, provided you use your training time well.

You'll find out a lot more about what that means as you read on, but it's worth establishing from the outset that there is no single "right" way of training for a triathlon. A former marathon runner, for example, wouldn't follow the same regime as someone with a low level of aerobic fitness but fantastic swimming technique. Someone new to the sport who just wants to "get through" their first race won't train in the same way as someone more experienced, looking to achieve a new personal best.

Tri fitness

That said, there are some key attributes that all budding triathletes need. Stamina comes top of the list. Whichever distance you race, you are likely to be on the move for at least an hour, which means you need to have a solid base of aerobic fitness. You can improve yours through any type of prolonged cardiovascular activity but, given that you already have three sports to contend with, it's best to use a combination of these to build your endurance. That way, your growing fitness is triathlon specific.

You also need to have muscular strength and endurance to be a good triathlete — in other words, muscles that can repeat the same action over and over without getting tired. (Think of the number of strokes you take swimming, the number of times you turn the pedals on the bike and the number of strides you take running.) Stronger muscles not only exert more force without fatiguing, they are also less susceptible to injury. But strength doesn't have to be gained by lifting weights in the gym: in fact, research indicates that working on strength within the activity itself is preferable — for example, pushing high gears on the bike

(overgearing) or running up hills. Good flexibility and core strength are also important factors, which is why regular stretching and strength training should be part of every triathlete's regime.

TRIATHLON RACE DISTANCES

Below are the main standard race distances you'll encounter. Some races are nonstandard, however, with distances that fall between these set categories. Beginners should set their sights on a supersprint or sprint to start with, to gain experience and confidence. Find out more about choosing races in Chapter Eight.

Supersprint:	0.25 mile (400 m) swim, 6.2 mile (10 km) bike, 1.5 mile (2.5 km) run
Sprint:	0.5 mile (750 m) swim (400 m in pool), 12.4 mile (20 km) bike, 3.1 mile (5 km) run
Olympic:	0.9 mile (1500 m) swim, 24.8 mile (40 km) bike, 6.2 mile (10 km) run
Middle Distance/Half Ironman:	1.2 mile (1.9 km) swim, 55.9 mile (90 km) bike, 13 mile (21 km) run
Long Distance/Ironman:	2.3 mile (3.8 km) swim, 111.8 mile (180 km) bike, 26 mile (42 km) run

The great divide

There's a lot to fit in, as you can see. So what's the best way of divvying up your time? Well, just as there is no set number of hours you have to train, there is no perfect ratio of running and biking to swimming. Even if we leave aside the matter of your personal talents and abilities within each (which will undoubtedly vary), the three sports are not equal. For a start, you don't spend the same amount of time on each during a race. A typical breakdown for a recreational triathlete might be 20 percent of overall race time on the swim, 50 percent on the bike and 30 percent on the run. To muddy the waters further, the training effect you get in one of the sports carries over to varying degrees to the other two sports. Research in the *International Journal of Sports Medicine* suggests that while to improve at swimming, you have to swim, there is far more crossover between biking and running. And also that biking will help your running more than running will help your biking.

So where does all that leave us? There are two crucial messages. First, the way you divide your time between swimming, biking, running and any supporting activities must be based on your own individual strengths and weaknesses. And second, you need to consider the overall importance of each discipline to triathlon as a whole before deciding to focus your efforts on it. For example, there wouldn't be much benefit in spending hours in the pool trying to reduce your swim time at the expense of cycling if there is clearly room for improvement in both — as the swim represents a much smaller chunk of the race.

One final clue as to how to allot your time stems from the age-old truth that we tend to neglect the things we aren't very good at! The ideal scenario is to improve your weaknesses while maintaining your strengths. To get a better idea of your personal starting point, grab a pen and jot down your answers to the following questions.

Determining your starting point

Are you currently regularly active?
If you haven't been active for a while, start gently and progress slowly to avoid pain and possible injury. You may want to check with your GP before beginning regular physical activity if you have been sedentary for more than six months or if you have existing health problems.

How would you rate your general fitness?
If you don't have a good level of aerobic fitness, concentrate on building this through steady-paced sessions using a mix of the three triathlon disciplines for six to eight weeks before beginning the training programs on pages 120–125, or any structured training program. It's a good idea to rely on your strongest discipline(s) at this stage, as you need to be able to maintain a steady effort for a prolonged period. (See page 119 for more information on how to rate your effort level.) If, for example, you are a poor swimmer, you won't get much aerobic benefit from flailing around in the pool for 10 minutes!

Do you already do one, two or all three of the sports involved in triathlon? Which ones are you good at?
It's likely that you already participate in at least one of the three "tri" disciplines, given that you're attracted to the sport. This will probably be your strongest discipline. The aim with training is to maintain your strengths while working on your weaknesses.

Within each sport, what are your strengths and weaknesses?
Looking more closely at each sport now, what are you good and bad at? For example, you might be good on flat bike rides but weak on hills, or good in pool swims but lacking confidence in open water. Chapters Two to Four will help you work on technique and skill within each sport.

Have you already done one or more triathlons? What were you good at and what could you improve on?
Racing isn't just about your ability within the three disciplines. It's about putting them

together seamlessly. That means performing under pressure, maintaining focus, executing smooth transitions and pacing yourself well. List the aspects of your race performance you would like to improve on.

Do you have any physical or mental barriers that are limiting — or could limit — your performance? (This could be a previous injury, a lack of nutritional know-how, poor core stability, or time constraints that will limit your training availability.)

It's not just ability that dictates how well we train and perform — consistent training, as well as supporting factors like good hydration and nutrition and injury prevention work count for a lot. Think of any factors that may hold you back and keep them in mind as you read on.

Going for goals

You should now have a better idea of your current position. But where do you want to get to? What is your goal? To complete or compete? You can have multiple goals, of course, but make sure that they don't conflict or create too much stress and pressure — learning to swim front crawl and compete in your first half Ironman race in one season could be excessive!

SMART principles

Now check your goals against the SMART goal-setting principles:

Specific: Have you outlined your goal in a detailed, specific manner?

Measurable: How will you know if and when you've achieved the goal?

Attainable: Is the goal yours and not set by someone else on your behalf?

Realistic: Is the goal challenging but achievable, taking into account any obstacles you identified in the previous section?

Time-framed: Have you set a time period in which you want to achieve the goal? Deadlines are very motivating!

So now you know your starting point and your desired finish point. Training is simply the method you use to help you move from

VOICE OF EXPERIENCE: RICHARD ALLEN

Goal-setting is an essential process. But goals don't have to be personal bests. Your goal could simply be to complete a race, to get through the run without walking, to speed up your transition or take on your first open-water event. As well as making sure your goals are SMART ones (see right), make sure they are compelling — that they encompass aims that you really want to achieve. A goal has to mean something to you in order for you to put in the commitment needed to achieve it.

one to the other. You'll find lots of information on how to devise a training program to ensure that you reach your goals safely and successfully in Chapter Seven, or you can follow one of top coach Richard Allen's sprint or Olympic distance programs (see pages 120–125). But whether you're swimming, biking, or running, every training session should begin with a warm-up and finish with a cool-down and stretch. Read on to find out why and how.

Warming up

There are two very good reasons to warm up before a workout. In fact, they are the primary motivators for any keen sportsperson: better performance and less risk of injury. A recent study at the University of Alabama demonstrated that an effective warm-up reduced the risk of musculoskeletal injuries (those relating to muscles and bones); research in the *Journal of Science and Medicine in Sport* found that an active warm-up improved athletic performance, while a pretraining stretch regime did not. Launch straight into your run, ride, or swim without a warm-up, then, and you're selling yourself short.

As well as physically warming up the body (making muscles more pliant and supple), warming up increases heart and breathing rates, enabling you to get more oxygen into the body and transport it to the working muscles more efficiently. The moment you begin moving, a signal is sent around the entire body to prepare for physical activity and it begins to make the necessary changes, such as increasing the release of enzymes involved in energy metabolism, diverting blood away from the organs and into the muscles and opening up more alveoli in the lungs to soak up more oxygen.

> ## HOT TIP
> You'll often see people stretching before a workout, but research shows that holding static stretches reduces your power output for about 1 hour, so it isn't advisable. You also risk tearing or overstraining muscles by stretching them when they aren't warm. A better approach is to mobilize the joints and then, if you feel the need to stretch, perform active or dynamic stretches (in which you move slowly in and out of the stretch). Alternatively, save the stretching for after.

The perfect warm-up can be divided into three key parts (but don't worry, we're still only talking about 10 minutes or so). The first part is about mobilizing the body, by gently taking the joints through their full range of motion through bending, extending and circling motions. These actions squeeze synovial fluid into the joints, lubricating their surfaces and helping to free up movement and minimize creaking and stiffness.

Mobilization

Even if your session is focused on one specific body area (for example, the legs in cycling) it's a good idea to mobilize all the joints unless you are very limited on time. Start at your head and work your way down to the feet. Perform each movement slowly and smoothly and repeat four times on each side or limb if appropriate.

Run through this head-to-toe mobilization routine at the poolside before you swim, before you get on your bike, or start your run or any other training session.

Neck rotations and side bends
Take your head in a gentle forward semicircle from left to right, allowing the chin to drop to the chest as it passes from side to side. Then drop the head directly from side to side, looking forward.

Shoulder rolls
Roll your shoulders forward, up, and back, using as great a range of motion as you can. Reverse the action, taking them back, up, and forward.

Rolldowns
Stand with your feet hip-distance apart and knees soft. Roll your chin to your chest and then allow the shoulders and arms to drop forward as you gradually lower your torso toward the feet, rolling down through the spine, bit by bit. When you have reached the floor, pause, then slowly roll back up to standing.

Arm circles
Take each arm in as wide an arc as possible to open up the shoulder joints. Reverse the action, or try one going forward and one back simultaneously to challenge coordination.

Side bends
Stand with your feet hip-distance apart and knees soft and allow one hand to slide down the leg, taking the torso directly to the side. Repeat on the other side.

Trunk rotations
Keeping the hips centered, rotate the head and torso to one side and then the other, but don't swing.

Hip rotations
With feet wider than hip-distance apart, draw an imaginary circle on the ground with your pubic bone, taking the hips through as wide a range of movement as you can. Reverse the direction.

Knee lifts
Standing tall, bring alternate knees up in front of you, keeping the opposite foot on the floor. Now take the feet up to the bottom, again keeping the opposite foot grounded.

Toe raises

Rise up onto your toes, pause, then lower back to the heels and repeat.

Ankle circles

Lift each foot off the floor and circle the ankle in both directions.

Raising heart rate

The second part of the warm-up is about raising heart rate and body temperature through gentle aerobic activity.

You can do this with a generic activity such as walking or marching in place (useful if you're heading off for a run on a cold, rainy morning), or you can make it more specific to the discipline you're about to perform — by swimming, cycling, or running at a very low intensity. Allow about 5 minutes for this stage.

Sport-specific activity

If you are really time-crunched, you could proceed with your session now without a problem. The third and final stage of the warm-up is perhaps best seen as the icing on the cake.

It's a way of switching on good technique and priming the right nerve-to-muscle pathways for the activity ahead. For that reason, it should be as specific as possible to the activity you are about to perform, perhaps incorporating some dynamic stretches (stretches in which you move in and out of the stretch position in a controlled manner) or drills (exercises that focus on one specific aspect of technique). You'll find drills specific to each sport in the next three chapters that you can incorporate into your warm-up. Now you're good to go!

Cooling down

When you've completed your training session, don't just stop your watch and head for the shower. In the same way that you gradually built up speed, you need to slow down little by little, rather than stop suddenly. This gives the body a chance to return to a resting state and reduces the chances of you suddenly feeling dizzy or nauseous. It also enables the recovery process to get underway, so you're less likely to wind up with sore, aching and stiff muscles. All you need to do is spend a few minutes (even 2–3 minutes makes a difference) running, swimming or cycling very slowly (pedal against a low resistance if you're on your bike), breathing deeply and putting almost no effort in.

By the time you've come to a halt, your heart rate should be approaching its resting rate, but your muscles will still be warm — making this the perfect time for a stretch.

Stretching

The aim of a post-training stretch is to help restore muscles to their resting length — the length they were before they were required to repeatedly shorten for an hour or more. These repeated contractions create tiny amounts of damage in the muscles, causing the long thin fibers they comprise to become tangled and misaligned. Stretching helps get the fibers realigned, preventing knots or regions of tightness from developing. If you don't bother to stretch, you run the risk of allowing this temporary shortening and stiffening to become permanent, which will have an added effect on joint function. For example, if the rectus femoris, a muscle in the front of the thigh that works hard in both cycling and running, tightens and shortens, it pulls the front of the pelvis down and tightens up the lower back.

Granted, a brief post-workout stretch won't actually *develop* your flexibility — that takes more dedicated effort and time investment (yoga, anyone?), but it will help you hold on to what you've got, which is important, when you consider that with every day that passes beyond our mid-20s, our innate flexibility deteriorates a little further! Soft tissue becomes more dehydrated as we age, decreasing joint lubrication and causing creakiness, while collagen fibers thicken and get stiffer. But regular flexibility training can attenuate this.

The bottom line, then, is that post-training stretching is the bare minimum you should do to retain a good range of motion across your joints, optimal length in your muscles and good musculoskeletal alignment.

Good stretching practice

Well, that's the "why" of stretching sorted. Now for the practicalities . . .

What? Always know what muscle or muscle group you are stretching. Make sure you maintain good posture and technique and that you don't tense up other areas while you focus on a specific body part (the shoulders are a classic area prone to this).

How? There are many different methods of stretching, with fancy names like active isolated, ballistic, and proprioceptive neuromuscular facilitation . . . but the most widely used, safe and convenient type for post-workout stretching is static stretching, in which you adopt the stretch position and hold it for a given length of time. When you do this, a stretch reflex occurs after a few seconds, as a result of the brain telling the muscle "It's OK, relax, we're not going to snap!" so you aren't fighting against yourself.

How long? Current guidelines recommend holding stretches for 20–30 seconds, repeating each stretch 2–4 times. According to research in the journal *Physician and Sportsmedicine*, this should be sufficient to maintain flexibility in most people. However, to extend your current range of motion and create a physical length increase in muscles, you need to hold stretches for closer to 2–3 minutes.

Bear in mind that flexibility varies from joint to joint and, to a degree, from person to person — the *Physician and Sportsmedicine* study found that some people needed to stretch some muscle groups (the hamstrings, for example) for longer to get results. If you find you have imbalances between left and right, stretch longer and more frequently on the tight side to redress the balance.

How far? Stretch until you feel tension, not pain, in the muscle. As the stretch reflex occurs and the muscle relaxes, you should be able to move slightly further into the stretch and hold again. But do not bounce in and out of your final position — that's like jumping up and down on an already-stretched elastic band!

How often? Stretch after every training session. Ideally, stretch all the muscles, but if you don't have time, the box below will help you focus on the major muscle groups you've worked.

Stretching routine

The sequence that begins opposite takes you through all the major muscles of the body. If you can do the whole thing, great — but if you're short of time, the key enables you to focus on the stretches most relevant to the activity you've performed.

● = *Swim*

● = *Bike*

● = *Run*

● ● *Quads*

Stand tall with feet parallel. Lift your right foot, taking your right hand behind you to grab it and bring it toward the bottom. Bring the pelvis into a neutral position (don't arch the back) and gently draw the foot in, keeping knees close together. It doesn't matter if your stretching thigh is in front of the supporting one, as long as you feel a stretch along the front of the thigh. Repeat with the left leg.

● ● *Hamstrings*

Stand facing a support between knee and hip height, such as a bench or chair. Extend one leg and place it on the support, with the foot relaxed. Your supporting leg should be perpendicular to the floor. Now hinge forward from the hips (keep the arch in your lower back), with the pelvis level and the knee of the extended leg straight. Feel the stretch along the back of the supported thigh. Repeat with the other leg.

● ● ● *Upper and lower calves*

Stand with feet a stride length apart, back leg straight and front leg bent, both feet pointing straight ahead. Press the back heel into the floor so that you experience a stretch in the "belly" of the calf muscle. Hold. Now bring the back leg forward a little, bend the knee and tilt the hips forward, so that the stretch moves down to the lower part of the calf and Achilles tendon. Now swap your legs around and repeat.

● ● ● *Hips/glutes*

Stand tall and cross your right foot over your left knee. Now bend the supporting knee and sit back, as if you were going to sit on a bar stool, keeping the torso upright. Keep the knee pointing out to the side and feel a stretch in the hip. Repeat on the other side by crossing the left foot over the right knee.

● ● *Glutes and hip rotators*

Lie face-up on the floor with both knees bent. Take your right foot across your left knee and thread your hands either side of the thigh and bring the leg toward the torso. Feel the stretch in the bottom. Repeat with the left foot across the right knee.

● ● *Side stretch*

Stand with feet below hip bones and arms by your sides. Drop the torso directly to the left side (as if you were sandwiched between two plates of glass), keeping the tummy pulled in. Feel a stretch along the right side. To increase the stretch, take the right arm over your head. Pause, then return to the start position and stretch to the right side.

●● *Upper back*

Stand with feet hip-distance apart and knees bent, clasp your hands together in front of the body, palms facing you and push the arms away from you, feeling a stretch along the back of the shoulders and upper back. Try to make your upper back into a C shape, as if you were resisting being pulled forward by your hands and knees.

●● *Chest*

Stand with feet hip-distance apart and clasp your hands behind you, palms facing each other. Keeping the shoulders back and down, draw the arms away from you until you feel a stretch along the front and sides of the chest.

● *Back of upper arm (triceps)*

Raise your left arm overhead and allow it to drop down behind your back. Now take the right hand up to the left elbow and gently push the left arm back until you feel a stretch along the back of that arm. Swap arms and repeat.

● ● ● *Shoulders (deltoids)*

Bring your left arm across the body, just below shoulder height and, using your right hand (holding above the left elbow), gently press the arm across the chest. Don't hunch the shoulder up. Swap sides and repeat.

●● *Hip flexors*

From a lunge position, with the left foot forward, take your right knee to the floor with the lower leg extended behind it (the knee well behind the hip) and shoelaces facing down. Tighten the tummy muscles and extend forward from the hips until your left knee is at 90 degrees. You should feel a stretch along the front of the hip joint and thigh. Repeat on the other side.

●●● *Lower back release*

Lie flat on the floor with knees bent and arms out to the sides level with shoulders, in "crucifix" position. Drop your knees to the left and head to the right, allowing your lower back to release, and hold. Now take the knees to the right and head to the left.

● ● *Upper body stretch*

Kneel down on the floor and take your bottom onto your feet, extending your arms out in front of you on the ground. Drop your head onto the floor and gently stretch from the fingertips to the tailbone.

● ● *Iliotibial band (outer thigh) stretch*

Stand tall, and then take your left foot behind your right and slide the left leg away from you. Keep your body aligned and reach your torso over toward the outstretched leg. Swap sides.

Now you know how to warm up, cool down and stretch properly, let's look at what you might be doing in between! The next three chapters will help you improve your technique and fitness in each of the triathlon sports.

CHAPTER TWO THE SWIM

The swim leg is the most frequently dreaded element of a triathlon. Many of us never progressed beyond school swimming lessons, and even for those of us who have hit the local pool since the turn of the century, triathlon swimming is quite a different ball game.

The main differences are that you'll be swimming in close proximity to a lot of other people (some of whom, it might appear, want to kill you) and, more than likely, you'll be swimming in open water rather than a pool. That means currents and waves, no ends at which to take a breather, no heating, no helpful black lines to keep you on course and no bottom to touch, if you get my drift. Oh, and to add to the whole challenge, you'll probably be wearing a wetsuit, too (more on that later).

Another factor that puts many people off is that triathlon swimming generally means front crawl (freestyle) rather than breaststroke. It's not illegal or wrong to swim breaststroke, but when you consider that in front crawl about 80 percent of the work comes from the back, shoulders and arms, while in breaststroke, the thighs and bottom are the major players, you can see why it might be prudent to opt for the former, given that these are the major muscle groups you'll be using in the other two disciplines.

If all this is making your heart beat faster already, don't worry. There's a lot you can do to build your confidence in the water, improve your technique and work on your swim-specific fitness and speed before the big day. But it *will* entail getting your hair wet a few times a week: swimming experts say that frequency is an important factor in improvement — so it's better to hit the pool two to three times a week for 30 minutes than to go for one long session. That's partly because it's such a technical sport — you can't simply push harder and expect to get better at it. As Terry Laughlin, founder of Total Immersion swimming says: "Swimming is a natural activity — if you're a fish." While triathlon swimming isn't markedly different from ordinary swimming, good technique is paramount in maximizing your race performance. Not only will it help you swim faster, it will also help you conserve energy for the next two legs. The fact that pro swimmers use 50 percent less oxygen to achieve the same speed in front crawl as untrained swimmers illustrates the point.

What is good swimming technique?

I was watching the swimmers in the fast lane at my triathlon club's swimming session the other night. Did they all have textbook perfect technique? No. Some seemed to glide through the water with little or no effort while others appeared to propel themselves with sheer force.

And that just goes to show that there's more than one way of swimming from A to B. But what are the main things to focus on in order to swim faster, more smoothly and more efficiently?

TRI TALK

Bilateral "To both sides," in relation to breathing.

Drag The force that resists our motion through water.

Drafting Swimming in another swimmer's wake to conserve energy.

Open water An outdoor body of water such as a lake, river or the ocean.

Sighting Lifting your eyes to see where you're going.

Time trial A timed effort to see how much distance is covered.

Windmilling Swimming with arms at opposite ends of the stroke.

PERFECTING YOUR FRONT CRAWL

Let the ankles be floppy, not rigid, during the leg kick. If you have rigid ankles, practice kicking with fins on. Their large surface area forces a greater range of movement.

Keep the legs straight, but don't rigidly lock the knee joints.

The upper body rotates — presenting a smaller surface area to the water, meaning less resistance — enabling you to extend your reach in the water and engage the latissimus dorsi (the strong back muscles), which span the entire back from the base of the spine to the shoulder muscles, rather than relying on the deltoids (the smaller and weaker shoulder muscles) to power your stroke.

Keep your feet close together (your big toes should be touching or almost touching) as your legs pass each other. Visualize yourself being slightly pigeon-toed.

The main role of the legs in triathlon swimming is to help you maintain a good body position, which can't be achieved if the legs are sinking and creating a dead weight. This is achieved through a swift — but not excessively energetic — leg kick. The kick should originate from the hips, not from the knees — if you only kick from the knees you increase drag and force your body position downward.

The core muscles in the trunk are engaged in swimming to prevent the back from arching and to facilitate the body roll as one unit (see page 163 for more on core training). It can help to focus on the direction your belly button is pointing as the body rotates.

Don't suck in too much air and make sure you breathe out slowly (rather than forcibly exhaling) while your head is in the water. Avoid holding your breath — otherwise you'll have to exhale and inhale when you turn your head and will end up gasping.

Keep your head still unless you are taking a breath. The waterline should meet your head somewhere between the top of your goggles and the crown of your head. This is partly dependent on how your body sits in the water. You may find that lowering or raising your head slightly gives you a better leg position. Think about looking forward rather than facing forward.

The hand should accelerate through the water as you move from the front of the stroke to the back — so it's a slow-to-fast motion. This helps you hold more water and gives you greater propulsion.

Pressing your chest down into the water sometimes helps achieve a streamlined, horizontal body position, particularly if you're heavy-legged.

Breathe to both sides in training, although you will probably find a single-sided breathing pattern works best in racing, as you need to get as much oxygen in as possible. If you always breathe on the same side, you'll use the arm, shoulder and back muscles on that side more and develop a muscular imbalance.

The whole of the forearm and hand are used in the pull — so the hand should stay in line with the wrist and forearm throughout the stroke cycle. A firm wrist will help increase the paddling effect of the hand, as the forearm becomes an extension of it.

Swim stroke step-by-step

According to Dan Bullock, director of triathlon swimming specialists SwimForTri, who contributed much wisdom and advice to this section, there are four key factors: correct arm and leg mechanics, stream-lining, distance per stroke and timing. Let's take it from the top . . .

Arm mechanics

Swimming is not as different from running as you might think. In running, you plant your foot and the body goes forward. With swimming, you "hold the water" and make progress via the body traveling over the hand. Good swimmers will hold more water and pull their bodies farther. Poor swimmers allow the hand to slip under the body without holding the water or gaining forward propulsion — rather like running on a treadmill!

To gain hold on the water, the hand should move from the front of the stroke to the back in a slow to fast motion. Too much power at the front of your stroke and the water you are trying to hold moves with the hand, as well as some slipping around the back of the hand. The more time you spend practicing, the better feel you'll get for it and the more you'll be able to prevent this. Let's look at the arm action from the point at which the leading hand enters the water and follow its movement through the stroke.

Entry

The hand (the right hand in this picture) enters the water at a point inside the shoulder line but not across the center line. The arm should be well extended (a long entry) but not straight — it only fully extends under the water. As the arm travels overhead toward entry, the elbow should be higher than the hand. If you slap the water on your entry, it could mean that your elbow is sitting lower than your hand or that you are entering with too rigid and straight an arm. A great exercise to correct this is the finger trail drill on page 37.

Glide

As the arm fully extends under the water, allow a slight pause before the catch (the next stage). This allows you to glide forward and will dissipate any air bubbles trapped around the hand caused by a sloppy entry. You are then able to pull against still, calm water when you start to catch, rather than the less dense mixture of air and water presented after a poor entry. This will help you hold the water more effectively and pull the body forward and over the hand.

Catch

The transition from the "arm-outstretched forward glide" to the pull is a key part of the stroke. It is the point at which the hand and forearm (the left in this picture) grip the water to pull the body forward. The elbow should remain bent and stay higher than the wrist and hand throughout this phase, with the hand closer to the midline of the body than the elbow. Some people describe the catch as like rolling your arm over a barrel or beach ball.

Pull

Now comes the pull, the part of the stroke that propels you forward as a result of the arm pulling the body over it. The arm accelerates throughout the movement right up to the point of exit, when the hand passes the hip. (It should be close to the body at this stage, for streamlining.) Keep the fingertips down throughout the pull phase.

Once the arm is pushing back (in other words, once the hand has gone past the elbow) the elbow begins to straighten and the angle of the wrist changes so that the palm is facing the end of the pool from which you came. A high stroke count is a telltale sign that your pull needs a little work. See page 42 to assess your stroke rate.

Recovery

Once the arm exits the water, the elbow immediately begins to flex again — staying high with the hand under the elbow. The body rolls toward the other arm, allowing more space for the recovering arm to clear the water as it travels overhead for re-entry. Don't keep your arm tense during this phase — this is your one chance to relax! If this recovery pattern sounds unfamiliar to you, you might be more used to seeing the swinging style of recovery, which is popular among triathletes, with hardly any elbow flexion and the arms recovering in a large circular motion above the waterline.

TRY THIS

Fists/Fingers drill

Purpose: To promote feel for the water and improve hold.

Swim your regular stroke, but on the odd lengths, make a fist with both hands and on the even lengths, spread the fingers out so that there are spaces between them. When your hands are clenched, it forces you to use the forearm to assist with your catch, as you can't grip much water with a fist. When you unclench your hand, you should notice a difference in pressure on your hand — use this feeling to keep your hand holding water as you move through the pull.

Finger trail drill

Purpose: To promote a high elbow recovery and to make you more aware of your hand position during recovery.

Swim your regular stroke, but during recovery, trail your fingertips forward through the water, slightly off to the side of your body, focusing on good body roll and keeping your elbows pointed up. If the body is fully rotated, the elbow will be in the highest possible position for the hands to clear the surface of the water. The flatter the body, the more immersed the hand remains.

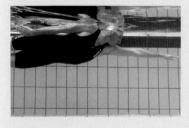

Doggy paddle drill

Purpose: To improve the catch and pull.

Just like Fido, you're going to keep your head up but your limbs under the water the whole time you swim this drill. Push off in a streamlined position, with both arms outstretched in front, legs straight, toes pointed and kicking lightly. Bend the elbow, keeping it high and use the right hand and forearm as a paddle to catch and push the water behind you (fingers pointing down). The hand should finish beside the hip — then the arm recovers under water, palm upward, back to the outstretched starting position. Repeat, alternating with the left arm.

DRILL TIME

Drills were invented to allow you to take out a specific aspect of the stroke, focus solely on that and then put it back into the full stroke.

Regular drilling is an essential part of becoming a better swimmer. And your progress will be even better if you can practice drills under the expert eye of a qualified swim coach. It's worth investing in a few one-on-one sessions or joining a swim club if you want to see results fast. (See Resources on page 172 for more information.) In the meantime, Dan Bullock, who demonstrates all the drills in this chapter, reveals how to get the best out of your drilling. He advises the following:

Quality, not quantity There is no point in practicing drills when you are tired or fatigued — all drills should be practiced over short distances with plenty of rest in between.

Be patient Don't try to rush things. The longer you spend trying to improve your stroke, the better the end product will be.

Mix it up Don't be afraid to mix up drills with normal swimming — half a length of a proficient drill is of more benefit then a full length performed badly. Swim the full stroke to complete a length if you swam a drill for the first half.

See the bigger picture When practicing a drill, concentrate on the aspect of the stroke it relates to — this will stop you from feeling overwhelmed by too many things at once. Then, when you return to full stroke, transfer the key aspects of the drill to it.

Do it often Try to practice your drills frequently. Four swims a week is ideal, even if it means the sessions are brief, as it reduces the lapse of time between sessions.

Leg mechanics

What about the legs? Well, kicking furiously isn't the way to go, especially for distance swimming and triathlons. Minimize energy expenditure by allowing the legs to work to balance the stroke and aid streamlining, rather than to keep you afloat or propel you forward, neither of which they do very well.

The kick starts from the hips, not the knees, and is an alternating upward and downward motion of the legs, with the ankles traveling just inches apart. Keep the depth of your leg kick within the profile of the body (in other words, don't let the legs drop too low) to reduce drag. As for kick speed, 2-4 kicks per stroke cycle is about right, but don't get too caught up counting — it's more important that your leg kick keeps you balanced and streamlined than that it adheres to any particular rhythm or pattern. It sometimes helps to focus just on the downbeat of the kick, not up *and* down.

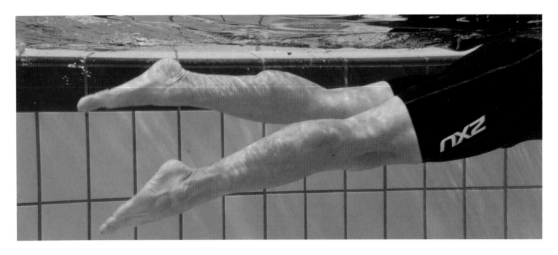

Streamlining

Now we know what the arms and legs are supposed to be doing, we can look at how to improve body position and streamlining. Being streamlined means presenting as small a surface area to the water as possible in order to minimize drag. If you imagine you are looking at a swimmer from the side, the body should be flat — the head, shoulders, back, hips, legs and feet being in alignment and parallel with the water's surface. Why? Because if your legs are too low in the water, they'll increase your frontal surface area and act like a brake, slowing you down.

While to a degree your body composition — the proportion of fat, muscle and bone — determines your body position in the water (fat floats better than muscle), an error in positioning is more likely to be to blame for poor streamlining. For example, holding the head too high is a classic cause of the legs being too low in the water — so experiment

TRY THIS
Kicking with a board
Purpose: To isolate and improve leg kick. Holding on to the front of a kickboard (buoyancy device) with your forearms resting on it, push off from the side and propel yourself forward using only the legs. Focus on good kicking technique (see page 38). Going forward means you are getting it right! A poor leg kick not only wastes a lot of muscle power — it can also hamper your forward motion, or worse still, make you go backward.

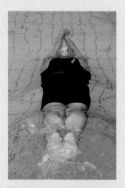

Push and glide drill

Purpose: To perfect your push-off and improve streamlining.

Push off from the side in a streamlined position — keeping the hands on top of each other, arms straight and outstretched, upper arms glued to your ears and head in a neutral position. Keep your body long and legs straight, toes pointed and don't let the legs sink. It can help to press your chest down against the water. Glide as far as you can and then swim the rest of the length.

Extension drill

Purpose: To improve body position, particularly when breathing.

Push and glide from the side, as above, and then swim with the lead arm outstretched, the unused arm trailing by the side, your upper body fully rotated so that the shoulder of the unused arm is out of the water. The shoulder of the lead arm should be rotated (palm facing down) and as close to the chin as possible — don't let the arm sink. Do six kicks in this position, then turn your head to take a breath. Avoid lifting the head out of the water to breathe — try to keep the lower lens of your goggles submerged and your head perfectly still when you aren't breathing. Practice alternate lengths to each side with a 30-second rest between.

Torpedo drill

Purpose: To improve body rotation.

Wear fins for this drill to maintain body position and allow the rotational movement to be performed more effectively. Push off on your back. While kicking, rotate your upper body from side to side, keeping the head perfectly still. Remember to take your shoulder to your chin, not chin to shoulder. You can also practice this drill on your front, holding your breath.

with your head position before you blame your muscle-bound cyclist's thighs!

The second crucial component of streamlining is body rotation. If you now imagine you're seeing a swimmer head-on, you would see the body rolling or rotating to roughly 45 degrees from side to side. Initiate the roll from the upper body and allow the hips to follow. Sometimes swimmers are taught to initiate the roll from the hips to give a fast, powerful stroke (for example, for sprinting) but it can throw you off balance and increases the likelihood of the arms crossing the midline when they enter the water.

The body should turn as a single unit — from head to toe — as if there was a skewer going lengthwise through it, like a kebab! This is far more efficient than swimming with your shoulders and hips square to the water. Not only will it minimize your frontal resistance (think of the shape of a submarine's nose — tall and narrow, not flat and wide) but it will also allow you to bring into play the stronger muscles of your back for a more powerful pull, automatically lengthening your stroke.

To prove the point, stand up and reach your arm overhead. Now rotate your body, keeping the arm lifted and notice how the hand extends farther overhead. The same thing happens to your stroke in the water. A good body roll also facilitates the turning of the head to breathe and assists with lifting the recovering arm and shoulder high over the water.

HOT TIP

Being wet from head to toe doesn't mean you're hydrated. Research in the *Journal of Strength and Conditioning Research* found that swimmers experience significant body fluid losses during training, which often go unnoticed due to the cooling effect of the water. Keep a bottle at the end of the pool during training.

Distance per stroke

This means exactly what it says. The more distance you travel per stroke, the fewer strokes you'll take per length or per race distance, thereby conserving energy. A longer stroke also creates more time to perform all the necessary actions required to swim smoothly. Take breathing, for example: a rushed, erratic stroke dictates when you breathe, often causing panic. With a longer, more relaxed stroke you create the time to breathe, so you feel less tense and panicky. Improving your distance per stroke isn't a matter of kicking harder — it's more a case of breaking the stroke down into its key parts and maximizing your efficiency in each part before rebuilding it.

Given that distance per stroke is such an important part of good swimming, knowing your stroke rate is a useful gauge of your current standard — and progress. Obviously, you don't want to be counting strokes on every single lap — but you could pick, say, every fourth lap to count. As well as giving

Catch-up drill

Purpose: To slow down and lengthen the stroke and maximize glide.
This is almost like swimming slow motion. Start your stroke as normal, but instead of performing the catch, leave the arm outstretched after entry and keep it there while the other arm performs the stroke, until it catches up with your stationary arm and they swap places. Any shortcomings in your catch and pull will soon be highlighted in this drill, as they cannot be masked by sheer force or momentum. Make sure that the outstretched arm doesn't sink while the other arm is performing the stroke. Perform this drill with a pull buoy between your thighs (see page 94) or without tools.

Exit drill

Purpose: This drill helps to make sure the hands are pushing all the way through to the back of the stroke. Place a kickboard between your legs vertically, as you would a pull buoy. Swim normally, but as you drive the arm backward, brush the float with the hand to make sure you are fully extending the elbow and finishing the underwater phase fully. This movement should make the back of the upper arm ache — and you should feel yourself surge forward . . . when it works! Do not sweep wide of the body with the hands; this will cause you to sway.

HOT TIP

Swimming with a pull buoy between your legs gives you a higher position in the water, more akin to swimming in a wetsuit — so it's a good drill to practice.

you a figure for your strokes per distance, this also enables you to assess whether your stroke count is staying constant or whether the figure is creeping up as you swim more lengths — an indicator that the mechanics of your stroke are tiring you out.

So what constitutes a good stroke rate? A good aim to begin with when you're starting out is 3 feet per stroke.

25 meter pool = 25 strokes per length
33.3 meter pool = 33 strokes per length
50 meter pool = 50 strokes per length

Don't cheat, though! Anyone can push off, glide and swim a length with an excessive kick between each arm stroke to get their stroke count to a minimum! Instead, aim for a sensible compromise between speed and a long, efficient stroke.

HOT TIP

Ever wondered if excess body hair is slowing you down? A study performed at East Carolina University on twelve swimmers found that shaving off body hair increased the distance traveled per stroke by a nifty 5 percent, probably because shaving decreases the drag on a swimmer's body. Go get that razor!

Good timing

Good timing is everything in swimming. It helps you maintain a streamlined position, stay relaxed and efficient, and maximizes your distance per stroke. If you're windmilling, with your arms working at opposites, you'll be expending a lot of unnecessary energy.

So what is good timing? You want one hand to enter the water just as the other begins pulling. That means leaving your arm outstretched in front for longer than you might expect to, which will help your streamlining and buoyancy.

Breathe while the arm is recovering, but make sure your head is back in the water before the hand makes entry — it's very common for novice swimmers to keep the head out too long, ruining the body position. When you breathe, don't lift your head right out of the water. If you watch good swimmers, it can appear as if they barely raise their head out of the water at all — this is because they are breathing into the trough that follows behind the bow wave that your progress through the water creates. Don't stop kicking — and certainly don't stop your arm action — when breathing. Everything carries on as normal. Take air in quickly and then return your head to a central position. Let the air out slowly during the stroke — keeping some air in your lungs helps to maximize your buoyancy.

VOICE OF EXPERIENCE: RICHARD ALLEN

Whether you're still mastering the basics or want to improve your speed and efficiency, it's essential to structure your time in the water, rather than simply getting in the pool and swimming up and down for a given time or distance. Breaking your session down into segments is not only more beneficial, it also makes it more interesting. Start with a warm-up of a few easy laps, perhaps including some pull buoy and kickboard work and then work on technique by performing some drills, depending on your specific weaknesses — and how soon your race is. When race day is still a long way off, work on your body position and stroke mechanics, but as race day draws nearer, it's good to practice some more triathlon-specific skills, such as sighting and drafting. It's worth focusing on one specific aspect of swimming when you are drilling — body rotation, for example, or breathing and timing. Don't just practice a random selection of unrelated drills. Once you've switched on your technique, you're ready for the main set — the bulk of your session in which you are working on your swimming fitness. But even this section should be broken down into intervals (unless you're doing a time trial) rather than swum as one long effort, as you'll see in my programs on pages 120–125.

Monitoring your improvement

Swimming faster and swimming a given distance in fewer strokes are sure signs that you are making good progress. Performing a regular time trial will help you assess the first. All you need is a stopwatch and the length of the pool. Swim for a set time — maybe 15 minutes to start with, building up to 30 minutes — and record how far you swim. This is known as a T15 or T30.

A fun way of monitoring your stroke efficiency is to play swim golf. After you've warmed up, swim four x 50 meters, timing each rep (50 meters) and counting your strokes. Take a minute's rest between each rep. (If you're in a 25-meter pool, count your strokes for each of the two lengths and add them together.) Combine the time it took to swim 50 meters with the number of strokes you took per length. As you improve, your handicap — your stroke count and speed — will go down. This helps remind you that speed comes from good technique. If you try to swim faster by taking more strokes, your handicap will go up!

Triathlon swimming

Working on achieving a more streamlined body position and a longer stroke will soon improve your speed and efficiency in the pool. But are there specific skills required for triathlon swimming? While the stroke remains essentially the same, you need to remember that maximum swimming speed per se isn't the prime goal in a triathlon — it's maximum speed bearing in mind that you still have the bulk of the race to get through afterward, which might better be described as optimal speed. To that end, you need to be doubly certain that you aren't powering the stroke with your legs, as you're sure going to need them for the next two disciplines!

You also need to make sure your wetsuit allows you a good range of movement so that your arms can extend and recover fully and your body can rotate (see page 98 for the lowdown on wetsuits).

But a far greater difference in triathlon swimming relates to the environment rather than the stroke itself. For example, the challenge of swimming in a large crowd, of negotiating choppy water, currents and waves, and of needing to see where you are going. Even pool-based events have their challenges and require some specific skills — such as a fast wall-turn and the ability to draft (see page 48). Plus, you won't have the bouyancy of a wetsuit and will need to count your own laps (which is why a 50 meter pool beats a 25 meter pool hands down). Let's take a closer look at the skills involved and how to acquire them . . .

Open-water know-how

While it's quite possible to work on some open-water skills in a swimming pool, there's no substitute for the real thing. Even just a couple of sessions will help prepare you for race day. There are an increasing number of venues — such as lakes and beaches — where you can practice open water swimming in a supervised session (see Resources, page 172, for details). In the meantime, it's also worth swimming in your wetsuit in the pool and practicing race-specific activities such as deep-water starts (see page 141), swimming two to three abreast and swimming around an

imaginary buoy. You can also use the pool to prepare yourself for some of the other challenges that entering the "washing machine" can entail. For example, you can learn to breathe on both sides, in case choppiness or the splashing of other swimmers leaves you with a mouthful of water every time you attempt to breathe on your preferred side. You can also practice drafting and work on your navigation skills.

Sighting and navigation

With no black lines to follow and wind or currents pulling you off course, it's easier than you might think to swim off-course

TRY THIS

Crocodile eyes drill
Purpose: To practice sighting.
Every six to eight strokes, look up and forward for three strokes, keeping the eyes just above the surface of the water. Exhale as you do this. Not raising your head too far will help stop your legs from being forced lower, creating drag. Do not attempt to take a breath while simultaneously lifting up to sight forward — inhale to the side as normal.

Swimming straight
Purpose: To avoid swimming additional distance.
If you can get a lane to yourself, practice swimming in the middle of it, keeping the black line directly beneath you. Try a few strokes with your eyes closed; if you continually veer to one side or the other, you should get your stroke checked out by a coach, as something will be out of balance.

WHAT TO WEAR

One of the biggest differences between a pool and open-water swim is your attire — a wetsuit versus a swimsuit or tri suit. If you are doing an open-water event and the water is less than 57ºF (14ºC), a wetsuit is compulsory. On the plus side, a wetsuit improves your buoyancy quite considerably — it's particularly helpful for people with a poor leg kick, as it reduces the amount of drag caused by trailing legs. But on the downside, it can feel alien if you're not accustomed to it — and if the wetsuit doesn't fit quite right, it can restrict your breathing and range of motion, particularly around the arms and shoulders. That's why it is so important to practice — you get used to the feeling of being clad in neoprene, as well as becoming more adept at putting on and taking off a wetsuit. Read more about finding the right wetsuit in Chapter Six.

during a triathlon, wasting precious time and energy in having to correct yourself. The best defenses against this are to practice swimming in a straight line and to sight efficiently. Sighting basically means looking where you are going — it's a good idea to pick a tall landmark on the shore and keep heading for it. The best way to do it is to look up every few strokes, keeping your head as low as possible — eyes just above the water.

The other options — stopping to tread water and peer around or swimming breaststroke while you get your bearings — are far more time-consuming and following someone else is a gamble not worth taking, as I can personally attest!

HOT TIP

You may need to sight twice in a row if the water is choppy or crowded to confirm your direction. Don't just go through the motions of sighting without actually looking at anything.

Breathing skills

Breathing bilaterally (every third stroke — alternately to left and right) will develop a symmetrical and streamlined swimming stroke. The added advantage of mastering breathing on both sides is that if conditions such as sun glare, chop or other swimmers demand that you breathe only to the left or right, you are able to do so. It's worth practicing bilateral breathing in all training sessions, even if you only breathe to one side during the race itself (which many triathletes do, in order to get more oxygen in). Breath-holding drills are good for strengthening the lungs and will also give you confidence if you're in a crowded start area and fear taking a breath and getting a mouthful of water or someone's elbow.

Drafting

Drafting — basically, gaining a tow in the slipstream of a swimmer close in front of you — can save you energy. A study from the University of St. Etienne in France found that drafting reduced drag by 13–26 percent, resulting in a 9.5 second improvement in 400 meter swim time. That equates to approximately 38 seconds over an Olympic-distance swim. While drafting is illegal during the bike leg of a triathlon, it's perfectly acceptable in the water and is well worth mastering.

In the pool or in open water, practice swimming level with another swimmer's lower legs — close enough to get the benefit of their speed, but not touching them. You do need to be right behind them to benefit, however.

TRY THIS

Bilateral breathing drill
Purpose: To build your confidence and ability to breathe to either side.
Breathe only to the left on the first length, only to the right on the second length, then every third stroke (bilaterally) on the third length.

Breath-holding drill
Purpose: To build lung capacity.
A good breathing exercise to try is to breathe every three strokes on one lap, every five on the next, building up to seven — or even nine. This will strengthen your breathing muscles and remind you to breathe out while your head is in the water. Novice swimmers often try to inhale and exhale when their face is out of the water and end up gasping for breath.

HOW TO DO A FAST WALL TURN

You can lose a lot of time in a race (or in training) by turning inefficiently. A tumble turn is the most efficient method, but a good wall turn can be just as fast.

As you reach the end of the length, look at the wall under the water and glide in with one arm outstretched.

Come in very close to the wall, rotate your body and sweep your legs into the wall, immediately turning to face the way you're going to swim.

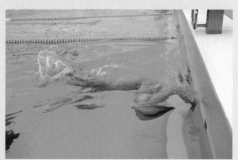

Push off the wall powerfully in an outstretched, streamlined position. Try to do all this in one smooth movement. Glide for a moment, but not for too long or you will start to lose your speed from the initial push-off.

You can draft — probably more effectively — by swimming directly behind someone, but swimming right on their feet can be quite daunting and it is much more difficult to do your own sighting with someone's legs kicking in your face!

Different strokes

Although front crawl (freestyle) is by far the most common stroke in triathlon swimming, you will inevitably encounter people swimming breaststroke, too.

Some triathlons, such as the London Triathlon, do not permit backstroke because of its similarity to the distress sign of floating on your back and raising one arm.

We've already looked at why breaststroke is not the ideal option, but you certainly shouldn't let an inability to swim front crawl stop you from entering a triathlon.

Swimming breaststroke in a wetsuit isn't as easy as swimming front crawl, because your movement is more restricted — so if you intend to do it on race day, make sure you practice it in training.

Breaststroking tips

Breaststroke is a leg-dominant stroke — with 80 percent of propulsion coming from the lower body, through the frog-like kicking action. Common errors include an uneven leg kick (screwkick), in which one leg kicks more than the other and an unfinished kick, in which the legs don't come back together fully after going out to the sides in the thrust phase of the stroke.

Many people put too much work into the arm action in breaststroke, driving the head out of the water forcefully and propelling themselves upward, rather than forward. You only need to clear the water line with your chin to inhale — don't lift your whole head out of the water, as this will drive your legs downward, increasing drag and putting excessive strain on the back. The other common error is taking the arms too wide during the opening phase — just beyond shoulder width is fine — and angling them downward rather than outward.

Finally, don't rush into the next stroke before you've completed the glide phase — which is "money for nothing" in terms of forward progression.

TRY THIS

Double kicks drill
Purpose: To work on your breaststroke kick, try doing two leg kicks for every arm pull.
This will help develop good timing, streamlining and stroke length. Simply swim one full stroke and keep your hands together in the outstretched streamlined position while you execute the second leg kick.

Kicking on your back drill
Purpose: To practice closing your leg kick in breaststroke. Push off the side on your back, with hands by your sides. Focus on closing the kick with force rather than whip-kicking the legs open.

CHAPTER THREE **THE BIKE**

Whether your cycling prowess is more on par with Lance Armstrong or with his granny, the bike leg of any triathlon takes up the biggest proportion of overall race time — so it is the area in which you can make the most meaningful improvements. While swapping your hefty mountain bike for a lightweight carbon frame is one way of shaving off minutes, there are many less costly techniques to employ.

The two main factors are improving your bike-specific fitness and working on your handling skills. Both are well worthwhile. Knock 2 percent off your swim time, for example, and it might amount to 90 seconds — knock 2 percent off your bike time and you may be looking at a 5-minute gain. What's more, it's much easier to brush up your cycling skills than it is to master perfect swimming technique. Granted, it's also easier to get away with riding a bike badly than it is to swim without finesse, but there is a price to pay for using sheer force over smart technique — a fact that many a triathlete has learned when they reach the run only to discover that their thigh muscles seem to have been replaced with concrete.

A third factor to take into account is your bike setup. Given that a bike is a fixed piece of equipment, if your position is wrong, it's your body, not the bike, that will adapt. This can reduce your power output and raise your risk of injury. According to bike-fitting specialists CycleFit, 99 percent of the people they test have a less than perfect setup. More on that later, but let's start by looking at riding technique.

NERVOUS AND NOVICE CORNER

If you're a nervous rider, start by riding in traffic-free areas, such as parks, on bike paths or even in empty parking lots. This will help you get used to your bike and build your confidence. Practice taking your hands off the handlebars, one at a time. Practice drinking from your bottle and then replacing it in the bottle cage without looking at it — it's looking down that is most likely to cause an accident. Practice tight turns. Even practice getting on and off your bike.

While you may not need to be proficient at negotiating traffic and other hazards in a race, you will need to face them in order to get the training miles in, so it pays to practice out there in the real world whenever you feel ready to.

TRI TALK

Aero bars Handlebar extensions (also known as tri bars) that allow you to adopt an aerodynamic position.

Cadence The speed at which you make your pedal strokes — or turn the wheels — measured as revolutions per minute (rpm).

Downshift To change to a lower gear — one that is easier to push.

Drafting Riding in the slipstream of another cyclist by staying close to their rear wheel to conserve energy. Drafting is illegal in the bike leg of all nonelite races.

Overgearing Pushing a heavy gear to build leg strength.

Spinning Turning the legs fast against little resistance.

Turbo trainer A piece of equipment that you mount your bike on, turning it into a stationary cycle, allowing you to train indoors.

Upshift To shift to a higher gear (smaller cog or larger chain ring).

HOW TO RIDE YOUR BIKE

Look where you're going, but make sure this doesn't cause you to overly compress the vertebrae at the back of your neck. Neck and back pain are among the most common overuse injuries in cyclists, according to a study in *Current Sports Medicine Report* — improper bike fit is one of the prime causes.

Keep your elbows bent and relaxed to absorb shock and prevent veering if you hit a bump. Keep your arms in line with your body, not splayed out to the side, to make you more aerodynamic and compact.

Your bike should be set up so that you are comfortable riding on the hoods — where you have maximum control and can change gear and brake easily. Keep your thumbs and a finger of each hand closed around the handlebars to prevent losing control of the bike if you hit an unexpected bump. But don't grip too tightly, and change your hand position frequently to prevent finger or wrist numbness.

In general, the ball of the foot should be directly over the center of the pedal axle to transfer maximum power to pedaling. Your cleat position should facilitate this. Riders with larger feet or calf/Achilles' heel problems, however, might want the pedal axle farther back behind the ball of the foot.

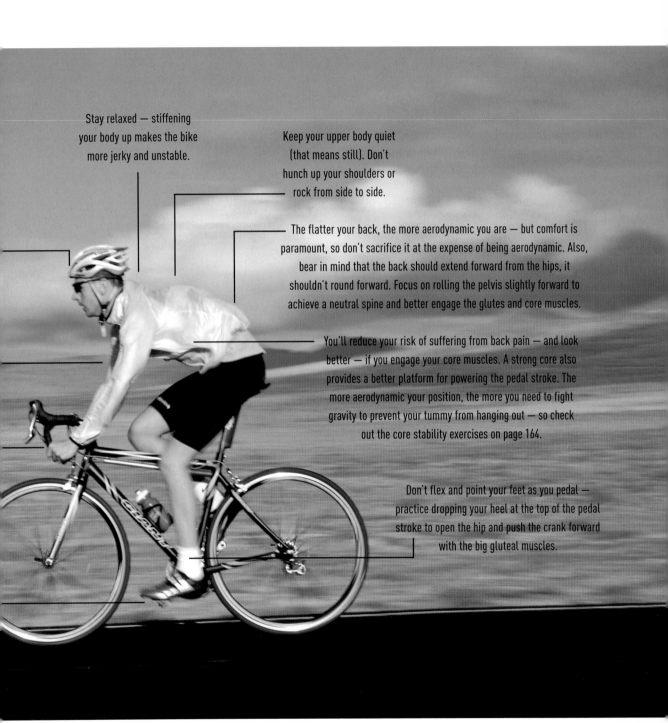

Stay relaxed — stiffening your body up makes the bike more jerky and unstable.

Keep your upper body quiet (that means still). Don't hunch up your shoulders or rock from side to side.

The flatter your back, the more aerodynamic you are — but comfort is paramount, so don't sacrifice it at the expense of being aerodynamic. Also, bear in mind that the back should extend forward from the hips, it shouldn't round forward. Focus on rolling the pelvis slightly forward to achieve a neutral spine and better engage the glutes and core muscles.

You'll reduce your risk of suffering from back pain — and look better — if you engage your core muscles. A strong core also provides a better platform for powering the pedal stroke. The more aerodynamic your position, the more you need to fight gravity to prevent your tummy from hanging out — so check out the core stability exercises on page 164.

Don't flex and point your feet as you pedal — practice dropping your heel at the top of the pedal stroke to open the hip and push the crank forward with the big gluteal muscles.

Mastering bike basics

The more time you spend in the saddle, the more comfortable and competent you'll become on your bike and the more familiar you'll become with how it responds to your handling — every bike is different. But time in the saddle isn't the only way to improve your cycling. Improving your core skills — pedaling, cadence and gear selection — will make a huge difference.

Cadence

Many cyclists get stuck in a rut with their gears — using just a handful of what's available rather than upshifting or downshifting in response to changes in the terrain. This often results in pushing too heavy a gear at a low cadence (see Tri Talk). While some cyclists stand firm on this approach to turning the wheels, Lance Armstrong revolutionized (excuse the pun) many a cyclist's approach to cadence when he made his comeback to cycling, riding at a pedal-blurring 100–120 rpm. Armstrong demonstrated that the way to travel faster is not to push a heavier gear but to push a smaller gear more frequently. In essence, this means you're spreading the workload over a greater period — using less force to turn the pedals. The upshot is you won't fatigue so quickly or put too much force on the knee joints (a force that can become seriously problematic if your bike setup isn't ideal and your knees are rolling in or out).

However, some research has shown that very high cadences lead to higher heart rate and quicker fatigue in some cyclists. And the evidence on cadence within triathlon is mixed. A study from the University of Bath found that a higher cadence during the bike leg produced a better run performance, although other research, published in the

VOICE OF EXPERIENCE: RICHARD ALLEN
A fairly high cadence — 80–100 rpm — will enable you to pedal smoothly and efficiently. Experiment to find what works best for you within these guidelines. This will be partly dependent on your body type, fitness level and the terrain you are riding on. Below or above the 80–100 rpm range tends to risk bringing in upper body movement and wasting energy unnecessarily.

HOT TIP
Recent thinking in triathlon is that for optimal efficiency and energy conservation, a cycle cadence that is half the cadence of your foot strike when running works best. For example, if you pedal at 90 rpm, you should run at 180 steps per minute. It's worth a try . . .

Journal of Sports Science and Medicine, suggests that it may be partly in the mind. In this study, a 65-minute cycle and 6.2 mile (10 km) run were used to simulate a triathlon situation and subjects were monitored using a fast, slow, and preferred cadence. Despite the fact that both the fast and preferred cadence bike legs led to faster running over the first third of a mile (500 m), there was no significant difference between *overall* run times for any of the three cycling cadence approaches. The faster cadences just made the run *feel* easier.

So, is there an ideal cadence? Well, in a study at the European University of Madrid, cyclists rode at a fixed power output at 60 rpm, 80 rpm and 100 rpm. Gross efficiency (economy of energy) was significantly greater at 100 rpm, compared to at 60 rpm, but only slightly greater than at 80 rpm. Muscle activity in the gluteus maximus (the butt) and vastus lateralis (a thigh muscle) was also lower at the higher cadences. This suggests that there is a range — rather than an ideal figure — within which you can get a good return on your efforts and that range lies somewhere around 80–100 rpm. Riders with big legs may find a lower cadence more efficient and it's also worth noting that women tend to cycle using a lower cadence than men. Experiment in training to find what works for you.

There are bike-mounted cadence monitors to help you monitor your rpms (see page 110), but if you're not in the market for another gizmo, then simply count the number of times one foot reaches the bottom of the pedal stroke in a 30-second period and multiply by two to get your cadence. Practice doing this at different speeds and using different gears to see how your cadence varies — the elites are able to maintain a steady cadence across different gears and terrains.

TRY THIS
Spin-ups
Purpose: To find your maximum comfortable cadence.
On an exercise bike, Spinning bike or turbo trainer, start pedaling at your usual cadence and increase it over a 30-second period to the maximum rpm you can maintain without bouncing in and out of the saddle. Maintain this maximum smooth cadence for a further 30 seconds and then return to easy pedaling for a minute. Try three sets of 4–6 repetitions, with a 3-minute easy spin between each set.

High cadence descent
Purpose: To work on increasing cadence out on the road.
On a ride, when you hit a gentle, steady descent, don't change to a higher gear but increase your cadence instead. Pedal as fast as you can to keep up — and only change gear when you hear that clunking sound that means you've lost it.

All change, please

Another gear selection issue relates to the angle between the front and rear chain rings. Basically, you're in the lowest gear when the chain is on the biggest cog at the back and the small one at the front and the highest gear when the chain is in the smallest cog at the back and the biggest at the front. What you *don't* want to do is be on the big cog at the back and the big cog at the front — or the small cog at back and front. This puts the chain at an extreme angle and it is far more likely to fall off. To make your gear changing smoother — and to prevent losing speed — try to unweight the pedals (shifting your body weight to the saddle to reduce the amount of weight pushing down on to the pedals) as you change up or down, especially when you're climbing a hill.

Incidentally, if you always find you end up with one of these extreme angle combinations, you might need to consider getting a different gear setup — for example, smaller or larger chain rings or an extra chain ring at the front (a triple).

One final thing to consider is *when* you change gear. A common mistake is changing gears too late. This is usually a result of not looking far enough ahead, so that you have to react too suddenly to obstacles or changes in terrain. Keep your eyes on the road ahead and you won't lose speed through this simple error.

> ### TRY THIS
> #### 90/10 pedaling drill
> **Purpose: To concentrate on a smoother pedal stroke with each leg individually.**
>
> **Working in a low gear, let one leg do 90 percent of the pedaling for 1 minute, then switch. Focus on making a complete pedal stroke and keeping it smooth. Practice 1 minute on each leg five to six times during your ride.**
>
> #### Single-leg drill
> **Purpose: To eliminate dead spots in the pedal stroke and improve glute engagement.**
>
> **On a turbo trainer or exercise bike with clipless pedals or toe clips, try five sets of single-leg pedaling for 20–25 pedal strokes on alternate legs. As you reach the top of the pedal stroke, try to drop your heel to open the hip and push down with more force from the glutes. This drill will reveal whether you have one leg working more than the other and will also highlight your weak spots during the pedal stroke — indicated by a clunking sound at the spot where you've failed to keep up.**

SEVEN WAYS TO GET THE BEST OUT OF YOUR BIKING

Get your bike set up professionally
A professional bike setup will ensure that your riding position is the most comfortable, safe, and efficient it can be (see pages 102–103 for more on this).

Structure your training
Getting out on the bike is good — but you'll reap more benefits, more quickly, if your training sessions have a specific focus. Check out the triathlon-specific training advice on page 66.

Do specific skills practice
It's worth spending time within some of your training sessions working on specific bike skills and drills. Focus on the aspects of riding you are weakest on.

Use clipless pedals
While being attached to your bike can be daunting at first, clipless pedals, which attach to cleats on the bottom of your cycle shoes, enable you to transfer more power from your muscles to your bike and, due to the stiffer sole of a cycle shoe, are more comfortable to ride in than sneakers. Toe clips, the cages that hold your feet in place, are another option, but unlike clipless pedals, they don't allow for foot placement adjustment. CycleFit recommends progressing from flat pedals straight to a clipless system.

Try to relax
Being too tense and rigid on the bike will make you ride less smoothly and fatigue more quickly. Try to keep your shoulders and arms loose and only have as much tension on the handlebars as you need to hold on. Try smiling!

Improve your core stability and flexibility
It takes good flexibility to achieve an aerodynamic riding position and good core stability to maintain it. But even if you're riding an upright bike, it's important to stay limber. Cycling is an unusual activity in that it only involves muscle actions that shorten muscles, none that lengthen. Without flexibility work, you'll end up with short, tight injury-prone muscles. Remember to incorporate the stretch routine from Chapter One. Research has also shown that a strong core can reduce the incidence of lower back pain, the bane of many a cyclist's life. Find out how to fine-tune your core stability in Chapter Ten.

Go spinning
Not the group exercise class (though that has its benefits) but pushing low gears at a high cadence. This will get your leg speed up (without bouncing), making you smoother and faster.

How to pedal

What? I hear you say. Pedaling technique? How hard can it be to turn the lousy pedals? Well, the answer is it isn't hard to turn them, but turning them smoothly and efficiently takes a little skill and practice. Compelling new research now suggests that the upstroke of the pedal stroke is passive, not active — a recovery from the downstroke, taking place while the other leg is pushing down. You can attenuate the potential loss of power by unloading the pedal during the upstroke, just after your foot has come round from the back, letting the force of the other leg's downward stroke do the work.

The only time when the upstroke — and the muscles that facilitate it, such as the hip flexors and hamstrings — becomes important is on steep climbs, when pulling up can provide extra traction.

While the pedals move in a circular way, the legs operate more like pistons, powering down during the downstroke and recovering during the upstroke. The amount of power exerted throughout the pedal stroke should *not* be constant, but it is possible to minimize the loss of power at the so-called dead spots of the pedal stroke (such as just before the top of the stroke). The best way to achieve this is to drop the heel at the top of the revolution, to open the hip and enable the glutes to engage during the downstroke. This leaves the quads less work to do and smoothes out the pedal stroke.

But don't get too hung up about which muscles do what. A study in the *European Journal of Applied Physiology* used magnetic resonance imaging (MRI) to monitor the pedaling activity of pro cyclists and found large differences in the level of activity in different muscle groups and in the muscular recruitment patterns used (what order muscles kicked in). The researchers concluded that there was no single correct way of executing the task of pedaling.

Improving your bike skills

Working on your cycling technique will have a huge effect on your efficiency. The next step is to hone in on specific riding skills — the kind you'll need for successful training and racing.

Climbing hills

The secret to successful climbing is gear selection and body position. Oh, and thighs like sides of beef.

Choose the right gear to get you up the hill before you hit the toughest spot — trying to downshift when the pedals are fully loaded risks the chain coming off or the gear slipping. Maintain a steady rhythm and don't stop pedaling.

If it's a long, steady climb, stay seated in the saddle for the most part and keep your hands on the hoods — a nice wide grip will allow you to keep your chest open so you can get as much oxygen in as possible. Look ahead, to the brow of the hill. Standing occasionally, even on long climbs, is a good idea as it slightly changes muscle loading.

For shorter, sharper climbs, you can power up by getting out of the saddle. Remember to change to a higher gear as you do this, as you will be applying more body weight through the pedals once you're standing. (That's why it's more energy consuming.) Holding the hoods, you can pull the bike from side to side, which increases the power you can push down on each downward stroke of the pedal. This is known as honking. Remember, it's the bike that's shifting weight, not you — and you don't want to swing it too much. It's common to see cyclists rocking from side to side as they struggle up a steep slope. Don't copy them. The other common mistake is to shift body weight to the front of the bike (in front of the saddle). This puts too much weight on the front wheel and slows you down, so stay back.

HOT TIP

If you find when you are pedaling that your bottom rocks from side to side in the saddle, it's likely that your saddle is at the wrong height. See "It's a Setup," pages 102–103, for information on how to get it right.

downhill riding safer and, perhaps, an incy-wincey bit faster.

First, don't pull up hard on the brakes when you realize you're going at 25/mph. This is just likely to make you skid. Instead, feather (press lightly on and off) the brakes. The front brake is more powerful on descents, as this is where most of your weight is, so squeeze it first (unless, of course, you're descending a very steep hill).

Lightly working the brakes in this way should enable you to slow down and control your speed during the descent, so that you don't have to continually comfort brake all the way down. If it's a very steep hill, take your weight right to the back of the saddle for improved stability and control. Keep the pedals stationary at three o'clock and nine o'clock. On the other hand, if it's a long, shallow hill, keep your legs turning to prevent them from stiffening up.

While the speed freaks' main concern on descents is streamlining, mine is not coming off my bike — so I stay on the hoods, occasionally sitting upright to let wind resistance slow me down. But if you're confident and competent on your bike, the fastest position for downhill riding is on the drops or on your aero bars if you have them and can see far enough ahead to be sure it's safe. The more horizontal your back, the greater your speed will be. But remember, you have to balance comfort and aerodynamics, while building your proficiency and confidence through practice. Oh and look where you're going.

Going down?

Hurtling headlong down a steep hill, the wind ripping tears from your eyes and whistling through your helmet — you either love it or you hate it. I'm one of the world's worst descenders, but I have, at least, learned a few techniques to make my

Taking a corner

You might find a pancake-flat race course, with no descents or ascents, but it's pretty unlikely you'll find one without corners — particularly as many races involve multiple laps of a particular circuit or straight.

Taking a corner badly can, at best, cause you to lose speed and time and at worst, see you kissing the tarmac. So how do you negotiate corners without going round the bend?

The first golden rule is to change into an appropriate gear for exiting the corner before you enter it (particularly important if the corner exits on to a climb). Slow down if you need to, by feathering the brakes. Visualize a line through the corner, bearing in mind that the shallower the arc, the faster you can go but the closer it will take you to the center of the road (not always a safe option). The second essential is to look where you want to arrive at — in other words, look through the corner.

This alone will improve your cornering instantly — you'll find that your body and bike will follow your head. Look to the point at which you will be exiting the corner and sail around without braking. If you panic and brake you'll have to work extra hard to get your speed up again on the other side of it. Depending on the sharpness of the bend, pedal softly as you take the corner or keep the inside pedal lifted. So, on a left turn, your right foot should be down by six o'clock, your left foot (the inside pedal) at twelve o'clock and vice versa. If you pedal,

you risk scraping your pedals against the ground due to the angle of the bike.

Stay balanced by pressing your foot down firmly on the outer pedal. Press your right inner thigh against your saddle to lean your bike into the turn and, if you're on the drops, bring your chest down toward the top tube to lower your center of gravity and enhance tire grip to the road. Once you've passed the apex of the turn, bring your bike to a more upright position and start pedaling again to gain speed as you exit the corner.

HOT TIP

If you do opt for a tri bike or fit aero bars to your road bike, don't spend more than 15–20 percent of total training time in the aero position. In this position, the upper body weight is taken through the upper arms rather than the core, so over time, adopting it too much can erode core strength and function.

Crowd control

If you are only just getting used to riding a bike again, it's worth trying to schedule in some training rides with others before your race, as cycling in close proximity to hundreds of other riders can be intimidating. Unless your debut triathlon

> ## HOT TIP
> **Novice pack riders should look at the back of the person in front, not the wheel, to avoid ground rush and panic-induced erratic riding.**

is a draft-legal elite event (in which case, you should probably be writing, rather than reading, this book) it will be illegal to ride in another cyclist's slipstream by staying very close to their rear wheel. This can conserve as much as 30 percent more energy than riding singly. That's why you'll incur time penalties if you do it in a race.

However, there's no reason why you can't draft in training — and it does help to build confidence on the bike. You'll learn a lot from others by observing their gear selection and handling skills and have a responsibility to cycle smoothly and predictably. If you're nervous about drafting mere inches behind someone's wheel or

RIDING IN TRAFFIC

For most of us, riding in traffic is a sad necessity of training. To maximize your safety you need to a) be confident and competent on your bike, b) ride assertively — but not aggressively, c) always assume that other road users are inattentive at best and d) follow the rules of the road. In other words, use hand signals before making maneuvers, don't jump lights and don't ride on the sidewalk.

- Don't ride right in the gutter edge — then you've got no room to move if a vehicle squeezes you over. It also makes it harder to pull out in front of parked cars.
- Be visible — wear bright colors and reflective strips and always use lights in dull or dark conditions.
- Ride straight — don't ride erratically.
- Practice keeping the bike in line as you look over your shoulder to make a maneuver — it's very easy for it to drift sideways.
- If you have to stop suddenly, try to have your feet horizontal and move your body weight backward over the saddle as you brake to prevent the back wheel from lifting off the ground.

about them riding on yours, you'll still benefit if you ride a few inches off to the side. And remember, even though you're riding in a group, you still need to look where you're going — so look beyond the rider in front to make sure you know what's coming, while keeping their back wheel in your vision.

In group rides, different hand signals are often used to indicate something important to the upcoming riders. For example, a hand pointing down at the road usually means there's something to avoid — a deep rut, a patch of glass or a slippery drain cover, for example. A raised hand is used to indicate that the group is going to stop.

If you get given a hand signal, pass it on to the riders behind you, too.

LONG LIVE THE TURBO TRAINER

It's cold and wet outside. There are white van drivers who want to kill you, pedestrians who actively invite collision as they step out in front of you, texting someone from their cell phone. Thank the Lord, then, for the turbo trainer. Mount your bike on this indoor trainer and it effectively becomes a stationary cycle, opening the door to focused, structured training. It's especially useful if you don't have access to long, uninterrupted rides. The fact that there are no downhills to take a break on means you get a more intense workout, minute for minute — and it's great for practicing drills. An hour's riding should be plenty. Remember to have water close by — the lack of air to cool you down can raise your body temperature quickly. Read more about buying a turbo trainer on page 112.

Structuring your cycle training

So much for skills and technique. But how do you actually go about training for the bike leg of a triathlon? In the race itself, you'll be riding at the fastest possible pace you can maintain for the given distance, taking into account the fact that you'll need to leave something left in the tank for the run. But that doesn't mean every ride you do should be undertaken at such a frantic pace. Including different-paced sessions in your program — some in which you cycle slower than you intend to in your triathlon, some in which you cycle at race pace and some in which you cycle faster (but not for as long) is far more beneficial. The longer-than-race rides are the most important, as they build a good base of endurance. The intensity is comparatively low, but that means you need to spend longer in the saddle to reap benefits. The goal is to get your longest rides up to one and a half to two times race distance (unless you're training for an Ironman!).

The shorter-but-faster rides are about building leg strength and power on the bike and should be performed as intervals of hard effort interspersed with easy spinning to recover. This could entail using hills, pedaling faster or pedaling against a high resistance without concern for cadence (known as overgearing). Perform these intervals at a harder intensity — or faster pace — than your goal race pace. A study published in the *Journal of Applied Physiology* found that interval training on the bike

(4-minute intervals at 90 percent effort, with 2-minute recoveries) improved cardiovascular fitness by 13 percent compared to sustained, moderate-paced cycling. Interval sessions are best done on an exercise bike or turbo trainer, so you don't have to worry about traffic or terrain. You can also incorporate drills into these sessions, to improve technique.

The third important type of training is race pace sessions — utilizing either time trials (your speed over a measured distance) or performing segments of your training session at race pace, but allowing recovery between them. For example, you might do an hour-long ride incorporating five sets of 5 minutes at race pace with a 1-minute recovery between each. Remember to start every ride with a warm-up and finish with a cool-down of easy spinning — and then stretch (see page 20).

CHAPTER FOUR **THE RUN**

Many a triathlon is won or lost on this, the final leg of the race. That might sound obvious, given that that's where the finish line is, but a recent study in the *International Journal of Sports Medicine* found that performance in the run was strongly correlated to final race result — in other words, it's hard to fare well overall if your run isn't strong.

It's not so much the distance that makes the run so challenging (unless you are entering a middle- or long-distance event, of course) — it's more the fact that you are running after already having pushed yourself hard through a swim and a cycle.

Research shows that the energy cost of running in a triathlon is higher than that of running without the prior bike ride — an Australian study even found that muscle-usage patterns differed. That's why prior experience of bike-to-run is so essential.

With practice, you'll be able to minimize that concrete leg feeling and, like the pros, you won't run much slower than you would if you were in a straight 3.1 mile (5 km) or 6.2 mile (10 km) race.

Running well

So what makes a good runner? A high level of cardiovascular fitness is essential, along with strong injury- and fatigue-resistant lower body muscles. Running is physically more demanding than cycling or swimming because in the latter two your weight is supported (by the water or the bike), while in running, you have to carry it from foot to foot. That's probably why running is the discipline most commonly associated with overuse injuries in triathlon (read about injury prevention in Chapter Ten). But just as important as your physical prowess is good running technique or form.

Good technique enables you to run with better economy (expending less energy for the same pace), effectively giving you more miles to the gallon as well as reducing your risk of injury. This chapter will show you how to work on both of these areas, before looking more specifically at running in a triathlon and what you can do in training to perform to the best of your ability on the day.

Arguably, running is the least technical of the three disciplines of triathlon. It certainly doesn't require the repetitious drills that swimming does nor the meticulous attention to detail that correct bike setup demands. But is there one correct way to run? It depends on who you ask. Some running coaches believe that there is indeed only one proper method of putting one foot in front of the other — others believe that there is room for individual differences and have a more "if it ain't broke, don't fix it"

TRI TALK

Cadence The number of times your foot strikes the ground per minute.
Gait Your style of running.
Lactate threshold The point at which lactic acid accumulates in muscles faster than it can be removed.
Recovery In the context of running, recovery is jogging really slowly (or walking if necessary) following hard effort in order to get your heart rate back down.
Tempo pace A swift, beyond the comfort zone pace.
VO$_2$ max The maximum amount of oxygen that can be taken up and used by the working muscles.

attitude to technique. In other words, if you're not having problems with your running or getting injured constantly, then stay as you are.

HOW TO RUN WELL

Don't bounce up and down as you run. You're traveling forward, not upward! Keep your head in line with your neck and spine and hold it still, but not rigid. Look ahead, not down at your feet, as this pulls the shoulders forward and causes the back to arch. Runners who look down at their feet tend to strike the ground more heavily.

Relax your shoulders — unnecessary tension wastes energy and restricts your movement. Keep your chest open to make sure you can get plenty of oxygen in and breathe however feels natural. You'll probably find that breathing through your nose is fine when you're jogging, but feels inefficient as soon as you pick up the pace.

Run tall, don't hunch over or bend forward from the waist and certainly don't lean back. Think Michael Johnson! It's good to keep your core muscles gently engaged (don't let your stomach hang out) but don't pull in the tummy too tightly or you'll pull the rib cage in and down, restricting breathing.

Bringing the heel up toward your bottom when the foot leaves the ground makes it easier to bring the leg through to the front quickly for the next stride. Visualize the area just above the back of the knee working to pull the foot off the ground rather than thinking about lifting your legs up in front using the quads and hip flexors.

Focus on getting your feet off the ground as quickly as possible — a glancing blow. There is no need to push off through the toes in order to achieve this — let gravity assist you.

Keep your wrists toned — not tense and not floppy. Relax your thumbs.

The arms counterbalance the movement of the legs and provide propulsion in running. Bend them to 90 degrees and make sure they track directly forward and back rather than traveling across the body (a slight crossing is fine, but don't overdo it). Moving your arms faster makes your legs move faster, so engage them more strongly when you're running hard, less when you are jogging.

When your spine is in a neutral position (neither overly arched nor rounded), your pelvis is level at the front and back, the optimal position for the muscles attached to it to work. If your back is out of alignment, the function and balance of these muscles is compromised and there is increased stress on the lower back.

When landing, keep the lower leg perpendicular to the ground, rather than extending it in front of you.

Don't run with rigid, flexed ankles. Let all the tension go when the foot is in the air.

Happy landings

The crux of the issue is where and how your foot strikes the ground. Increasingly, many experts suggest that we should land with the ball of the foot directly beneath the knee. Landing on the heel, with the foot far out in front of the knee, they argue, acts like a brake, slowing you down and forcing you to work hard to regain speed with every stride. It also increases the impact forces that are sent up through the body, raising injury risk, say the forefoot proponents.

According to research in the journal *Medicine & Science in Sports & Exercise*, a forefoot strike creates a smaller stride, as the foot is landing below, rather than in front of your center of gravity. Given that you're covering less ground with each stride, you therefore need to take more strides by increasing your cadence (steps per minute). One way of achieving this is to focus on getting your feet off the ground as quickly as possible, flicking your heels up toward your bottom. You may also find that a slight forward lean (from the heels, not the waist) helps — by enabling you to work with, rather than against, gravity.

I'm not suggesting that forefoot striking is the only way to run well, however. In fact, a recent study in the *Journal of Strength and Conditioning Research* looking at foot strike patterns among 415 elite runners at the 9.3 mile (15 km) mark of a half marathon found that three-quarters were rearfoot strikers. When I saw this study, I huffed to myself, "So much for elite runners all being

forefoot strikers!" but on closer inspection of the finish times of the race participants, I noticed that a greater proportion of the non-heel strikers finished faster.

What about injury risk in relation to foot strike? I consulted Dr. Irene Davis, a biomechanics expert and director of the Davis Lab at the University of Delaware. "Different foot strike patterns result in different loading patterns on the lower limbs and are associated with different injuries," she told me.

This is borne out by the study in *Medicine & Science in Sports & Exercise* mentioned earlier. The study found that landing on the ball of the foot significantly reduced loading of the knee, but that the ankles worked harder. Davis's own research has shown that a heel strike creates loads that are more associated with stress fractures in the shinbone, while a forefoot strike is associated with a greater risk for Achilles tendinitis. "More of the cushioning is done by the ankle and calves in a forefoot strike," explained Dr. Davis. "So if you're predisposed to Achilles or calf problems, your injury risk may increase rather than decrease." What's more, who's to say the increased number of landings you make with a higher leg turnover (literally, moving your feet faster) won't raise injury risk?

Time for a change?

And there's something else to consider: the notion that changing your technique could actually raise, rather than lessen, injury risk. Physiotherapist and running expert Alan Watson says we have to take into account why we run the way we do. "The body compensates for its imperfections, and the way you run may be an adaptation to your gait abnormalities," he says. Watson regularly sees people in gait analysis whose technique he would expect to predispose them to certain injuries, but who have remained injury-free because, he believes, they have built up the necessary strength and flexibility to avoid such problems. "Changing one aspect of the gait will necessitate another alteration elsewhere," explains Watson. "If we are biomechanically designed to work in a particular way, then changing it could cause excessive forces to be built up elsewhere, leading to increased injury potential."

Taking all this into consideration, it seems that the jury is still out on the best way to run — leaving you to make your own call on whether you want to try to change your foot strike pattern. If you do, be prepared to invest some time and effort. Remember, it may have taken you decades to build up your current running style, so you aren't going to master a new one in a matter of weeks. See Resources on page 172 for information on specific running techniques and their supporting books and DVDs, and page 109 to find out how to make sure you are wearing the correct running shoes.

Regardless of whether you're up for revolutionizing your foot strike, most of us could do with sharpening up our style a little.

Even seemingly little things, such as running with tense shoulders, a waggling head or too much bounce, can have a negative impact on your running. See how your form compares to the image on page 70.

Getting better

Simply paying more attention to your body position will alert you to errors in your running technique. I like to run through a regular body scan — a sort of head-to-toe check — to see if I'm holding any unnecessary tension or slumping or arching my back, for example. Dr. Davis also recommends listening to your stride, which can provide valuable feedback — if you can hear your feet pounding the ground then you're not running as efficiently and smoothly as you could be.

What about stride length and cadence? The research suggests that as far as getting faster is concerned, increasing cadence, rather than stride length, is the way forward — particularly if you have a relatively slow leg turnover (below 170 spm). You can assess your stride rate by counting each left footfall over a 1-minute period and then multiplying the figure by two. A decent stride rate is considered to be 180+ steps per minute — Paula Radcliffe's is 194! If you could do with speeding yours up a little, set a handheld digital metronome to a rhythm that is a couple of beats faster than your current stride rate and work to the beat. Gradually raise the figure by two beats as you become accustomed to moving your feet faster.

Run to the hills

Hill training is another way of enhancing your running technique, not to mention your leg strength. While the hill increases your cadence and shortens your stride (preventing you from overstriding), the resistance you encounter recruits more muscle fibers and builds strength. It also taxes the cardiovascular system, as you have to lug your body weight uphill! Any undulating run will give you the benefits of hill training — or you can run repeats up and down a particular hill. For the best training effects, opt for a fairly long, steady gradient rather than a short, near-vertical slope.

Not all hill training is about climbing, however. Running down a slight decline enables you to work on increasing your leg turnover with less resistance. But don't overdo either the steepness of the hill or the number of reps you do — downhill running puts a lot of stress on the muscle fibers, due to the high proportion of eccentric muscle contraction involved and can cause considerable muscle soreness up to forty-eight hours later.

TRY THIS

Running drills

Another way of improving your technique is to incorporate some drills into your run sessions. Just like with swimming, these drills each hone in on one particular aspect of the gait pattern. By perfecting each individual stage, you enhance the whole.

The drills below will help to establish the neuromuscular pathways needed for running well. They will also contribute to your leg strength and speed. The ideal time to do them is as part of your warm-up. Aim for three to four sets of 50 to 60 feet for each drill.

Foot-plant drill

Run with a high cadence and short stride, picking your feet up quickly and bringing them close to your bum on every third step (so that you're swapping from left to right each time) and landing with the foot below the knee, not out in front.

Crossovers

Running is a unidirectional activity — you go forward 100 percent of the time. This means some muscles work a lot harder than others. Crossovers engage some of the non-running muscles, work on movement speed and challenge coordination. Stand sideways and take one foot in front of the other to travel laterally. Then go back in the other direction, leading with the opposite foot.

High skips

Skip from foot to foot, emphasizing the explosive action and lifting the knee up in front but landing with the foot below the knee. Use your arms as if you were running.

Fast feet

On the spot, pick your feet up as quickly as possible — as if there were hot coals on the ground. Use your arms to help propel you. Once you've got the rhythm going, move forward.

Training smart

Improving your technique and strengthening your running muscles will certainly help you become a better runner. But you still need to train smart. Training isn't just a matter of going out running at the same pace for the same distance, a few times a week. Each of your sessions should have a specific focus, helping you build on your existing ability to take your fitness to the next level. But don't run before you can walk. Research reported in *Sports Injury Bulletin* found that the two biggest culprits in running injuries were sudden increases in volume or intensity and doing too much — not technique faux pas. That's why it's so important to increase your mileage and speed slowly but surely.

If you are new to running, a great place to start is the beginner's program on page 83. Even if you're already aerobically fit through another sport, you still need to allow plenty of time on your feet for your body to get accustomed to the specific demands of running. And then you'll be ready to tackle the unique challenge of running in a triathlon.

VOICE OF EXPERIENCE: RICHARD ALLEN

Practice running off the bike on a regular basis. If you're new to triathlon, it doesn't have to be a formal brick session — you could simply perform a ¹/₂ mile run after every bike ride. When you are more experienced, you might want to link an easy run to a harder bike ride every couple of weeks. The more you struggle with the sensation of running off the bike, the more frequently you should practice it. It also gives you the opportunity to perfect your transitions!

Triathlon running

It's often said that triathlon running is not a question of how fast you run, but how little you slow down. The two key issues are that your biomechanics (the way your body moves) will be slightly different, given that you've just got off the bike and that you'll be somewhat fatigued before you start.

The two main aims in training, therefore, are to get comfortable with running the distance you need to cover in the race (and ideally, farther) and to get accustomed to running off the bike.

Let's start with running the distance. For a sprint or Olympic-distance race you'll be covering 3.1 miles (5 km) and 6.2 miles (10 km) respectively, at the fastest pace you can muster. But, as with cycling, that doesn't mean every training session should replicate this. In fact, you'll get far better results by incorporating some runs that are longer than race distance (overdistance runs) and some that are faster than the pace you'll be running on race day. The way to make this achievable is to make the longer runs slower than race pace and the shorter runs faster. You can also up the ante by mixing bouts of effort with periods of recovery (slow jogging or even walking), through fartlek or interval training. See pages 80–81 for three key sessions to try.

As for the second issue — running off the bike — well, research conducted at the University of Colorado found that running after cycling resulted in a smaller stride length and a greater stride frequency in the

TRY THIS
Bike-run brick
Purpose: To experience and get accustomed to the bike-run transition sensation through multiple repetitions.

Warm up and then cycle at your race pace for 10 minutes (6 minutes for sprint racers) followed immediately by an 8-minute run at race pace (5 minutes for sprint). Rest for 3 minutes and repeat. Build up to three repetitions. You can also do this kind of brick session in a gym, using an exercise bike and treadmill.

initial stages of a triathlon. But as the run progressed, stride lengthened out and frequency decreased — while overall speed increased. This demonstrates that elite athletes, through training, have managed to minimize the effects of fatigue and the altered biomechanics resulting from the bike and swim. And you can bet your bottom dollar that brick sessions are their secret.

Building bricks

A brick session simply means a session in which you practice more than one discipline — most commonly biking and running. For newbies, the focus of brick sessions is to get used to the transition many times over rather than using a long bike ride, long run format. Don't worry about speed at first, but gradually build up to race pace. There's no point doing them all at a jog, as this won't help you on race day.

HOT TIP

Race pace doesn't equate to a specific heart rate or speed, as that depends on the race distance and your own experience, aspirations and fitness. I always think of it as the hardest pace I can sustain for the distance — which would obviously make my marathon race pace a lot slower than my 3.1 mile (5 km) race pace. One way of gauging your race pace, if you don't yet have a triathlon under your belt to go by, is to do a single-discipline race equal to the distance of the run in your triathlon — such as a 3.1 mile (5 km) or 6.2 mile (10 km) — and use your heart rate or effort level rating as a basis for your training sessions. See Chapter Seven for more information on gauging pace and effort level.

THREE KEY RUNNING SESSIONS FOR TRIATHLETES

1. Overdistance run

OBJECTIVE

To run farther or longer than race distance or time at a comfortable pace (significantly slower than your expected race pace), to enhance aerobic fitness and stamina and give you confidence.

THE DETAILS

The exact distance/duration of the run depends on your goals, fitness and preference. If you're a beginner, you need to allow time to work up to race distance and beyond. On the other hand, if you are a keen and competent runner, be aware that doing too many sessions longer than 90 minutes will be of little benefit to your overall triathlon performance, hampering your recovery and reducing your training time and potential in the other disciplines.

TRY THIS

Run for 30–90 minutes, picking up the pace for the last 5 minutes. This is when you'd be getting tired in a race and practice gets you accustomed to the sensation of speeding up rather than slowing down as time progresses.

2. Tempo run

OBJECTIVE

To run at a swift, "beyond the comfort zone" pace for a sustained period, in order to increase what's known as your lactate threshold (LT).

THE DETAILS

The LT occurs when lactic acid — a by-product of intense exercise — can't be flushed out of the muscles as quickly as it is being produced, allowing it to build up and cause trouble. When this happens, your muscles feel like giving up and you'll be gasping for breath. Running at a pace that puts you close to this point teaches your body to raise the threshold, so that in time, you can run faster without crossing it.

TRY THIS

Aim to run for 15–30 minutes at tempo pace or do three to five 6-minute intervals with a 2-minute recovery in between.

3. Interval training and fartlek

OBJECTIVE

To train faster than race pace, by interspersing hard efforts with recovery periods.

THE DETAILS

Short efforts with long recoveries improve your VO_2 max (the maximum rate at which oxygen can be extracted from the air and used by the muscles) and power, while short efforts with short recoveries increase lactate tolerance, leg strength and the ability to work anaerobically (without oxygen).

TRY THIS

Ten reps of 1/4 mile at 3 mph pace (400 m at a 5 km/h) (a fast pace you can sustain over 3 miles) with 90-second recoveries. If you feel tired halfway through, slow your pace rather than increase the length of the recovery period.

If you've never tried interval training before, start with the less structured option, fartlek. Like interval training, you can manipulate variables to focus more on speed, power or endurance but the idea is to keep moving — just changing pace to vary effort. You can use the topography and terrain of the landscape (urban terrain works just as well) to dictate where you change pace or you can use blocks of time.

TRY THIS

5 minutes at tempo pace, 20-second sprint, 5 minutes easy. Repeat three to four times.

SEVEN WAYS TO RUN BETTER OFF THE BIKE

Practice it in training
Brick sessions will help you get accustomed to the feeling of running straight off the bike so it won't feel so alien.

Get your legs moving
As you reach the end of the bike leg, change to an easier gear and spin your legs more quickly. It can also help to stand up out of the saddle, to allow the legs to straighten and the calves to stretch.

Start with a full tank
The smartest place to fuel up for the run is when you're on the bike — taking on fluid and energy, in the form of gels, drinks or bars. This ensures that you don't begin the run dehydrated or energy depleted. See Chapter Nine for more on fueling up.

Watch your cadence
Don't push high gears on the bike — as you learned in Chapter Three, this will just leave your thigh muscles fatigued. A study from Colorado demonstrated that run times after fast-cadence cycling were as much as 10 percent faster than run times after slow-cadence cycling.

Don't fight it
Be mentally prepared for those first few strides when you'll feel as if running is a skill you haven't quite mastered yet. Accept it and wait for your running legs to return.

Do the quick step
Take short, quick strides as you begin the run. Your leg muscles will be tight from cycling, so big strides aren't advisable. Think of your feet landing underneath your body, rather than extending your lower legs out in front.

Save something
Always remember that the run is coming — if you give your all on the swim and bike then you'll have nothing left for the run, no matter how well you've trained.

Beginner's Run Program

If you're new to running, this eight-week program of four training sessions per week will start you off on the right foot. By mixing walking and running, you will progress safely and comfortably to a point at which you can jog for 30 minutes. This will stand you in good stead for the triathlon training programs in Chapter Seven. Note: in the table x4 means repeat the whole set (both running and walking) four times.

SESSION	1	2	3	4
WEEK 1	run 2 mins walk 3 mins x 4	run 2 mins walk 3 mins x 5	run 2 mins walk 3 mins x 4	30-minute brisk walk
WEEK 2	run 3 mins walk 2 mins x 4	run 3 mins walk 2 mins x 5	run 3 mins walk 2 mins x 4	35-minute brisk walk
WEEK 3	run 4 mins walk 2 mins x 5	run 4 mins walk 2 mins x 6	run 4 mins walk 2 mins x 5	40-minute brisk walk
WEEK 4	run 5 mins walk 1 min x 5	run 5 mins walk 1 min x 6	run 5 mins walk 1 min x 5	jog 10 mins walk 10 mins jog 10 mins
WEEK 5	run 7 mins walk 1 min x 4	run 7 mins walk 1 min x 5	run 7 mins walk 1 min x 4	jog 10 mins walk 10 mins jog 10 mins walk 10 mins
WEEK 6	run 9 mins walk 1 min x 4	run 9 mins walk 1 min x 4	run 9 mins walk 1 min x 4	jog 20 mins
WEEK 7	run 10 mins walk 1 min x 4	jog 20 mins	run 10 mins walk 1 min x 4	jog 25 mins
WEEK 8	run 15 mins walk 2 mins x2	jog 25 mins	run 15 mins walk 2 mins x2	jog 30 mins

CHAPTER FIVE **THE FOURTH DISCIPLINE**

Transition — the progression from one discipline to the next — is popularly described as triathlon's fourth discipline. It may not require physical fitness, but with the clock still ticking as you get out of the water and onto your bike and off your bike and into the run — speed, skill and know-how are essential. Think of all the hard work it takes to knock 30 seconds off your 6.2 mile (10 km) run time. Well, simply sharpening up your transition could save you that with no training at all and earn you a faster finish time.

I witnessed a great illustration of the importance of good transitioning while watching a race at Dorney Lake, near Windsor, England. The lead swimmer exited the water minutes before anyone else. "Great swim," I called as he jogged toward the transition area (the switchover location). But despite the considerable run to transition, he hadn't even got hold of the zip of his wetsuit by the time he arrived at his bike. A few fumbling moments followed before he clumsily pulled off the wetsuit, sat down to put on his bike shoes and fiddle with his GPS watch. By this time, his valuable lead was lost and I was yelling myself blue in the face from the spectator balcony! To avoid making a similar mistake, there are three things to think about: good planning, efficient multitasking and, perhaps most important, practice.

Setting up

Good planning entails setting up your transition area before the race in a logical and organized manner. Most races will allocate you a specific spot in the transition area (or at least a specific bike rack), though some are more of a free-for-all, allowing you to set up wherever you like.

ELASTIC FANTASTIC

Triathletes who start the bike ride with their shoes attached to the bike use elastic bands to keep them the right way up. This stops the shoes from dragging along the ground when running with the bike, which could cause them to fall off. It also keeps the shoe up the right way once you've mounted, which makes it easier to slip your foot into. When your foot is inside the shoe and you're pedaling normally, the elastic bands will snap. So how do you do it? Thread the elastic band through the heel loop of your shoe (if they don't have a heel loop, secure the band around the entire shoe) and attach the other end to your bike's frame. To determine where to attach it you need to decide which shoe/pedal you want in the front — if you are scooting, you'll want the nearside shoe at the front, but if you intend to hop over the saddle, you'll want the shoe farthest from you forward (see page 89 for more information on mounting techniques). The front shoe is best attached to the drink's bottle cage on the seat tube and the back shoe can be looped over the quick release skewer or rear-mech screw. Most triathlon-specific bike shoes have a Velcro strap, which you can leave open.

Your bike

Start by racking your bike on the horizontal bars provided. Hook the nose of the saddle over the bar, handlebars facing toward you, so that you can remove it easily and it will be facing the right way to steer out of transition. Make sure you leave your bike in a low gear so you can pedal freely out of transition. Now hang the strap of your bike helmet over the brake hoods or balance it between your tri bars — making sure the straps aren't twisted. If you are using eyewear, place the glasses inside the helmet, up the right way to grab and slip on, with the arms open.

It's a good idea to lay your gear out on a towel in the order in which you'll need it — use a distinctive or brightly-colored one and you'll be able to locate your spot a lot easier. Put the towel on the same side you want to be standing in order to rack and unrack your bike, to save having to go around the other side. It's worth noting that most races don't allow you to use extraneous items to mark your transition spot — such as hanging a flag or balloon from the handlebars or sprinkling talc on the floor.

Your shoes

If you are wearing bike shoes in the race, you have two options:

1. Put your bike shoes beside your bike. Place them toward the back of your towel, facing the right way, so you can wipe your

feet off without stopping to dry them properly before stepping into them.
2. Attach your bike shoes to the pedals. See the panel opposite to find out how to do this.

If you are wearing running shoes for the bike ride and run, your job is simpler, as you only have one set of footwear to think about. Place them at the back of the towel, facing the right way to slip on. Make sure the shoes are open nice and wide, tongues out, so you don't have to bend down and fiddle around to get them on. This is where elastic laces come into their own — fumbling around with laces when all the blood is rushing around your legs is no easy task!

Other gear

If you are taking a drink on the run or wearing a hat or visor, leave these beside your running shoes so you can grab them as you stand up to go.

Once you've got everything you need for the race set up, clear away the clutter. Your transition bay should not look like a hotel room, with bags and towels everywhere! The less mess there is, the easier it will be to locate what you need and get on with your race.

That's the transition area itself sorted. Now let's look at the process of transitioning — and how you can speed it up while remaining efficient. The mantra here is "more haste, less speed" — there is no point in trying to do two tasks quickly if you can't even do one of them smoothly.

T1— swim to bike

The transition from swim to bike is called T1 and it starts at the point at which you reach dry land. As soon as you've found your feet, put your goggles up on your head and locate the zip cord of your wetsuit so you can start unzipping it as you jog or walk back to the transition area. Don't take your goggles off (unless it's a non-wetsuit swim), because it's difficult to get a wetsuit over your hands with a pair of goggles in them.

Desuiting

Keep moving as you remove first one arm and then the other from the wetsuit and then push it down firmly to hip level. Leave it in this position until you reach your bike. Then lose your swim cap and goggles and standing on your towel, pull the wetsuit down in one fell swoop to well below your knees. Stand on it with one foot as you lift the other leg up high so you can use your hands to pull the fabric over your ankle. Then stand on the free leg of the wetsuit to help get the other one off. Experienced triathletes will already be putting

HOT TIP

Covering your ankles and lower legs, forearms and wrists with baby oil helps ease the passage of your wetsuit over these areas. If you find your wetsuit is very tight at the wrists and ankles and tricky to remove, trimming down the sleeves and legs can help.

on sunglasses and fastening their helmets as they take off their wetsuits — but don't do this if you intend to put on any additional clothing over your tri suit for the bike ride (ever tried to get a T-shirt over your head with a bike helmet on? I have!). Do, however, make sure you have your helmet on and fastened before you put your hands on your bike.

Footwear

As for your shoes, if you're wearing sneakers, put them on now. If possible, avoid wearing socks, which just eats into your transition time. Some talc sprinkled along the insoles will help absorb more moisture. If you must wear socks, pre-roll them so you can just stick your toes in the ends and roll them up.

Of course, the advantage of wearing running shoes is that once you've put them on in T1, you don't need to waste any more time on footwear in T2. The disadvantage, though, is that the relatively soft sole doesn't maximize your transfer of power to the pedals and can make your feet sore. That's where bike shoes come in. But these, too, have pros and cons — primarily to do with when and where you put them on. The advantage of putting your bike shoes on before you mount the bike is that you don't have to mess around trying to put them on while in motion. The disadvantage is that they are very difficult to run in and on slippery surfaces, quite hazardous. The advantage of attaching your bike shoes first is that you can run to the mount line in bare feet, saving time and reducing your risk of taking a tumble. The disadvantage is that you then have to ease your feet into your shoes on the move. This takes practice and is particularly difficult if you are faced with an uphill climb out of transition (see the following page for some tips).

Whatever footwear and method of bike mounting you intend to use, make sure you've practiced it in training enough times to feel comfortable doing it on race day.

Once you're appropriately clothed, grab your bike helmet, put it on and fasten it before you even touch your bike. Moving your bike without a secured helmet usually incurs a time penalty or worse, disqualification. All the same advice stands for a race with a pool swim, though you'll have the advantage of not having to free yourself of neoprene in T1.

Mounting your bike

Once you are ready to leave your transition area and head for the bike exit, push your bike with one hand firmly on the saddle, not by holding the handlebars. This gives you much more control and stops you from banging your legs into the pedals. Look in the direction you want the bike to go to help yourself steer.

Once you have passed the race mount line you are allowed to get on your bike. Again, there are a number of options.

If you are wearing running shoes, all three of the following options are viable. If you are wearing bike shoes, but want to put them on in transition (as opposed to attaching them to your bike), you should go for option 1 and if your shoes are already attached to the bike, go for option 2 or 3.

1. Stop the bike just beyond the mount line, get on and going (clipping in, if appropriate).

2. Scoot, which means transferring your hands from the saddle to the handlebars and putting your foot on the nearside pedal and then pushing off from the ground with the other foot on the same side, before lifting the leg over, once you've got some momentum. (Again, look where you want to go and the bike should maintain a straight course.)

3. Take the handlebars and tilt the bike toward you, swinging your leg over so that the inner thigh makes contact with the saddle. Then push or hop off the supporting leg and put both feet on the pedals.

Once you're on your bike and in motion, T1 is over — but you may still need to get your feet into your shoes. Try to keep looking ahead as you get hold of the back of the shoe and lift your foot off and inside in one smooth movement. Do up the strap, then pedal again to get your speed back up before repeating the process on the other side. Don't rush getting your shoes on — it's more sensible to wait for a suitable time and place. If it's a climb, don't even attempt to get them on until you reach flat ground or better still, a slight downhill, so you don't lose too much speed as you freewheel. It may be a little while before you actually get your feet in your shoes, so definitely practice cycling with your feet on top of shoes.

Then you should be on your way!

T2 — bike to run

The transition from cycling to running begins at the dismount line — the line beyond which you must be off your bike to avoid incurring penalty points.

Dismounting

Again, there are different dismounting options. The easiest is simply to stop the bike before the dismount line and get off. You can do this whether you are wearing running shoes or bike shoes. It's straightforward and foolproof (as long as you remember to unclip!) but it isn't the fastest way.

A better option is to use a cyclocross style dismount. To do this, you bring your right leg over the saddle and thread it between the left leg and the bike frame so that the right foot hits the ground first. This enables you to dismount without stopping and break immediately into a run, saving time. If you are wearing bike shoes, you need to unstrap them and get your feet out well before the dismount line, cycling with your feet on top of your shoes. This is especially important if the final few yards are uphill, where you won't be able to freewheel to undo your shoes.

When you're off your bike, take hold of the top of the saddle again, to push it back to your transition area. Once there, hang your bike on the bike rack using the brake hoods (to save turning it around) in the designated spot. Only when your hands are off the bike are you allowed to remove your helmet.

If you cycled in running shoes, you're good to go — taking any drink, hat or sunglasses that you might want with you.

> ## HOT TIP
> **As soon as you are into a good rhythm of cycling, take a drink. You'll need to rehydrate after the swim.**

Changing shoes

If you wore bike shoes, you now need to get into your running shoes as quickly as possible. To do this, put one hand on the tongue of the shoe and one on the heel tab and with the shoe as open as possible, slide your foot in. Some triathletes smear a little petroleum jelly at the back of the shoe to ease the foot in. It's best to get your shoes on standing up rather than sitting down on the ground, as standing up quickly after exertion can make you feel dizzy. Again, you'll save time if you can forgo socks, but remember to preroll them if you're determined to wear them. Now you need to make your way to the run exit area. You're on the home stretch!

Transition is something that few triathletes practice — so getting quick and efficient at it can really give you a leading edge. There is more information on how to execute smooth and speedy transitions on race day, when it really counts, in Chapter Eight.

TRY THIS

Transition training drill

This bike-run transition drill comes courtesy of Richard Allen, who teaches it in his training camps. Purpose: To practice and perfect what you intend to do on race day — so don't get hung up about how fast you run or cycle.

WHAT YOU NEED

Bike, helmet, eyewear, bike shoes, running shoes, socks (if you are wearing them), stopwatch.

SETTING UP

Find a wide-open space with a smooth tarmac surface and room for you to set up a transition area and a mount/dismount line around 80 feet from it. You also need space to cycle a 300–600 feet loop. Ideally, do this drill with a partner, who can time you and look after the transition area or even act as the bike rack!

Do the entire drill in running shoes if you intend to wear them on race day; otherwise, set up your bike shoes on or beside your bike. It's easier to attach your shoes to the pedals by mounting the bike and clipping them in than by trying to clip them in using your hands. Rig up your shoes using elastic bands, as shown on page 86 and make sure you've left your bike in a low gear.

Set up your helmet, sunglasses, running shoes and socks as you would in a real race transition area.

HOW TO DO IT

Begin at your mount/dismount line, approximately 80 feet from your transition area. Time yourself from the moment you start to run toward your bike. Get your helmet on as quickly as possible, fastening the strap before you touch your bike. Run back toward the mount line, pushing your bike by the saddle and when you've passed it, mount either by stopping, scooting or hopping on.

Once you're on the move, ride your short bike loop (300–600 feet). If you started with your shoes attached, try to get them on as you ride, without veering off course or coming to a standstill! You may want to complete two laps, to give yourself time to get your feet in and then back out of your shoes by the time you reach the dismount line. When I'm removing my shoes, I like to hold the shoe level at the back until I've secured it with my foot on top, to stop it from swinging round on the pedal and either causing my bike to stall or the shoe to fall off.

Once you've dismounted, push the bike by the saddle back to your transition area before getting your running shoes on as fast as you can and running a lap of the bike route. Stop the clock! With practice, you should find your time for this drill coming down.

CHAPTER SIX **THE GEAR**

So now we come to what I like to think of as the fifth discipline of triathlon — shopping! But don't worry if you're not a fellow shopaholic — there really is no need to spend a fortune on all the latest apparel and equipment — particularly when you're just starting out in the sport. In fact, doing so risks being branded with the dreaded "all the gear and no idea" label! This section looks at the essentials for each discipline, as well as optional training tools and race-specific gear.

Swim gear

The two basics are swimwear (trunks or a swimsuit) and goggles. A swim cap is optional — wearing one will minimize drag, particularly if you've got long hair and helps you retain body heat — particularly important in open water. It's also compulsory in many races, as a form of identification.

Swimwear

The most important factors with swimwear are fit and comfort. Women should make sure the torso of the suit is long enough so that it doesn't pull down on the shoulders and that the straps don't chafe or rub. Guys often have an "over my dead body" policy about Speedos, but it is worth bearing in mind that voluminous board shorts will increase drag — making a compromise between the two is the best solution (at least until your tri-perfect body emerges). Both sexes should look out for long-lasting fabrics, such as Speedo's Endurance, which retain shape better and resist the damaging effects of chlorine.

Goggles

Goggle choice is a very personal thing. Try on lots of pairs before deciding what to go for, as different brands and models work better for different-shaped faces. The acid test is to see if the goggles hold fast to your eye sockets for a couple of seconds without the strap. You shouldn't have to overtighten the strap in order to hold them in place — if you do, you'll probably end up with leaks — and panda eyes.

It's worth having a couple of different pairs of goggles for different conditions. Many triathletes, including myself, opt for a hybrid goggle/mask combo, which offers a greater visual area and better peripheral vision. Lens color is also a consideration. Blue tinted lenses reduce glare from light reflected off water, while brown or orange tinted lenses improve contrast.

If you wear glasses, it's worth thinking about getting prescription goggles if you're going to be taking your swim training seriously. Speedo, Zoggs and Aquasphere all offer prescription options. See Resources, page 172, for details.

See Resources, page 172, for details.

TRI TALK

Aerodynamic Reducing wind resistance.
Cleats Clips that you attach to the sole of bike shoes.
Clipless pedals Pedals that attach to bike shoes via cleats.
Tri suit A one- or two-piece outfit designed specifically for triathlon.
Wicking Drawing moisture away from the body.

HOT TIP

Don't rule out buying secondhand triathlon gear. E-bay, bike shops and triathlon magazines are worth checking out.

Swim tools

There is a whole range of swimming tools that you can use to help you focus on different aspects of your stroke. The drills in Chapter Two should give you some ideas of how to use them.

Kickboard

No prizes for guessing that this flotation device is designed to help you focus on your kick. For the best buoyancy, hold it at the leading edge with your forearms resting on the board. Bigger swimmers need bigger kickboards, so shop around.

Pull buoy

A pull buoy is a flotation aid shaped loosely like a figure eight. You place it between your thighs to keep your legs afloat while you focus on what your arms are doing. Swimming with a pull buoy gives you a good feel for body rotation and is useful for drills like catch up and finger trail. Again, larger swimmers should look for larger floats.

HOT TIP

Place the pull buoy as high as possible — if it's down near your knees it's harder to hold in place — and don't kick! Keep your feet together and pointed.

Hand paddles

Paddles can be used to work on strength or to hone technique — particularly the movement of the arm through the water. They attach to your hands with straps to create a greater surface area with which to stroke.

Paddles should be used sparingly, because the increased resistance they offer can increase the load through the shoulder joints — particularly stressful if your technique is not 100 percent perfect. The resistance also slows down stroke rate, which is not something you want to make a habit of. That said, paddles can help you get a feel for the catch and the slow-to-fast movement of the arm through the water.

Many swim coaches recommend removing the wrist straps to better reveal faults in your stroke mechanics.

Fins

Fins (a.k.a. flippers) help to improve your kick, add speed and stability to your stroke and work on ankle flexibility. Opt for short-bladed ones rather than diver-style long ones. The stiffer the blade, the greater the ankle flexibility needed — or the greater the ankle flexibility you'll develop over time. Fins are great to wear for some drills, such as single-arm drills or side kicking, as you don't have to expend as much energy just trying to stay afloat.

HOT TIP

Do some warm-up lengths before you put fins on — otherwise the sudden transition to an enforced pointed toe position can result in a cramp.

Wetsuits

If you're going to be racing in open water, you'll need a wetsuit. A wetsuit designed for swimming is not the same as a wetsuit designed for, say, surfing or waterskiing, in which the main aim is to give protection and warmth. The difference is in the flexibility and thickness of the neoprene. For swimming, you need optimal flexibility, particularly around the shoulder area and a suit that moves with you like a second skin. Swim-specific wetsuits don't come cheap, but if you aren't convinced that you want to take triathlon seriously you can always rent one for the season with an option to buy at the end of your trial.

Regardless of whether you are buying or renting, correct fit is essential. Try on lots of suits before you commit and if at all possible, test them in the water. At the very least, move your arms around in a swimming action to assess the suit's flexibility. Buying a wetsuit online is risky if you haven't tried it in a store somewhere first — at least check the Web site has a suitable returns policy. See Resources on page 172 for more details.

Getting it on!

Even if your wetsuit is the perfect size, it won't be any good if you don't put it on properly. It's quite common to see people at races with the crotch area of their wetsuit hovering somewhere just above the knees! If this is the case, then the suit will be pulled downward and you won't get the range of movement you need at the shoulders. Allow plenty of time to put your wetsuit on.

Start by applying liberal amounts of baby oil to your ankles and calves — some people slip a plastic bag over each foot to ease the suit over. Get the foot and lower calf of each leg of the suit into the right place and then roll the neoprene over the top of this area and pull it up from the inside. This helps prevent you from tearing it and assists you in getting the panels in the right places. Continue to do this all the way up to the hips, rolling the neoprene down over the area you've already positioned and reaching down on the inside to pull it up. Now put some baby oil on your wrists and forearms and begin the same process with each arm. Remember, it's the armpit and shoulder area where fit really counts.

Once you've got the suit on, you can bend each limb in turn to create a fold of fabric to pull up if necessary. Do this with each knee and elbow and at the torso by bending forward. If your wetsuit is difficult to get off over the heels and hands, consider trimming the arms or legs down a little so that the ends are wider and easier to remove.

SEVEN TIPS FOR CHOOSING THE RIGHT WETSUIT

So what is correct fit? Mike Trees, a former pro triathlete, gives the lowdown.

1. Look for a suit that is snug, but not restrictive.

2. Make sure the arms below the elbow are particularly tight fitting to prevent water from flushing into the suit. The neck should also fit snugly, but not feel as if it is strangling you.

3. Get the torso length right — too short in the torso and it will put pressure on your shoulders, too long and you'll get air bubbles inside.

4. Be picky about size. Many wetsuit brands (including 2XU and Blue Seventy) offer as many as 10–15 sizes per model, so you should be able to find something that fits you correctly. If not, then a custom-made suit is an option (see Resources, page 172).

5. Weigh up flexibility and buoyancy. The more buoyant a wetsuit, the less flexible it is — so you have to strike a balance. Entry-level wetsuits generally increase flexibility by using strategically placed thinner fabric, while more expensive suits use more high-tech, flexible materials. Look for thinner neoprene on the shoulder area and armpits to allow for greater flexibility.

6. Make sure you can get in and out of the suit relatively easily. A long zip allows for easier removal but may let more water in and slow you down. It also tends to mean the suit is less flexible, as the zip obviously doesn't stretch.

7. Once you've found the perfect wetsuit — look after it. Rinse it in plain water after use and allow it to dry naturally — not in direct sunlight or on a radiator. Store it flat or hang it on a hanger rather than rolling it — or, horror of horrors, leaving it stuffed in a crate!

Your bike

If you are in the market for a new bike, you are well positioned to make sure that what you buy is suitable for your training and racing and fits you perfectly. If you already have a bike and don't want to buy a new one, it's a matter of making the most of what you've got — either by tinkering with the bike's setup yourself or having a professional fitting.

Does your bike need to be triathlon-specific? The short answer is no. In fact, tri bikes are designed for racing and are not ideal in nonracing situations (such as training on busy roads), primarily because of issues of comfort and safety. Many people compete at a good level in triathlon on a standard road bike. So how do the two differ? The key difference is the position the bike puts you in due to the length of, and angles between, various parts of the bike. For example, a tri bike has a shorter top tube and a steeper seat-tube angle, which opens up the hip/torso angle rather than compressing the hips by folding the body.

On a road bike, your weight is distributed 60 percent to the rear, 40 percent over the handlebars. On a tri bike, it's more like 60 percent to the front, 40 percent to the rear which, while giving you a flatter, lower, more aerodynamic position, also makes the bike less stable to handle. Being on tri bars (aero bars) also puts you out of reach of the brakes, which isn't safe for riding in traffic.

As a starting point, the best advice is to opt for a road bike, to which you can later attach tri bars and go-faster wheels.

HOT TIP

Give yourself time to adjust to changes to your bike setup — and make changes in small increments, rather than whacking your saddle up by 3 inches in one go!

SEVEN THINGS TO CONSIDER WHEN YOU BUY A ROAD BIKE

1. Size and fit are crucial — never buy a bike without test-riding it and get professional advice about the correct frame size and setup.

2. Do you feel comfortable in the riding position? While lots of components of a bike are adjustable, the frame itself is not — and this has a strong influence on the overall riding position.

3. Does the bike handle in a way you are comfortable with? A shorter wheel base (the overall length of the bike) makes a bike twitchier than a longer wheelbase, for example.

4. Bear in mind that the frame is the most important aspect of your investment, as you can upgrade the components attached to it later on (or you may even be able to get the shop to swap components for those better suited to you, such as a woman's saddle or narrower handlebars).

5. Women should consider a woman-specific bike, designed for a shorter body and longer limbs, relatively speaking. But it's not the only option — some women fit men's bikes better.

6. Consider a triple chain ring if you'll be tackling a lot of hills or if you lack leg strength.

7. Think about the weight of the bike — most entry-level road bikes will be aluminium framed, perhaps with carbon forks and seat stays. Full carbon or titanium frames cost a lot more. Expect to spend around $750 for a decent entry-level road bike.

IT'S A SETUP!

Handlebars: Bar width should be equal to shoulder width. Err on the side of a wider one, though, to open your chest.

Handlebar height: Don't put your handlebars so low that the drops are uncomfortable to use. Yes, it might be more aerodynamic but it's no good if you stay on the hoods all the time.

Saddle to handlebar drop: This is typically no greater than 3 inches for a road bike, up to 4 inches for a triathlon bike. Anyone with neck pain is advised not to use big drops, which may exacerbate the problem.

triandrun.com

Saddle level: The saddle should be level, though a slight downward tilt is OK if it's more comfortable. It is often more comfortable to angle the saddle down if you are using aero bars.

Saddle height: Your knees should be slightly bent at the bottom of the pedal stroke and your hips shouldn't rock in the saddle. As a starting point, aim for a 30-degree bend at the knee. A good indication of correct saddle height comes from putting your heel onto the bottom pedal when the pedals are at six o'clock. The leg should be straight, so that when you then put the ball of your foot on the pedal, you get a slight bend at the knee.

Saddle fore-aft position: Check that your knee is lined up over the ball of your foot on the pedal. The tibial tuberosity, a bony prominence just below and on the outside edge of the knee, is a good marker. Now reach forward with a neutral spine (don't arch or round) so you can contact the bars without rolling the shoulders too far forward. Try to take your hands away without pitching forward. If you can't, shift the saddle forward a little.

CUSTOMIZE YOUR MOUNTAIN BIKE FOR TRIATHLON

A few relatively inexpensive changes can make your mountain bike fit for the roads.

• The most important change is the tires. Lightweight road tires or slicks, will enable the wheels to roll much faster than bumpy mountain bike ones. You'll need 26 inch-diameter tires for a mountain bike, 1–1.5 inches thick.
• Take off any unnecessary weight, such as mudguards and pannier racks.
• If the bike has lock-out suspension, lock it on the roads to prevent wasting energy.
• Adding tri bars will enable you to adopt a more aerodynamic position. Or add bar ends to give you more options with your hand positions.
• More fundamental is to replace the chain rings so you can go faster on the flat and downhill. Go for a large chain ring with at least 50 teeth.

Bike gear

Once you've bought (or adapted) the bike itself, here are some essential pieces of gear to consider adding to your shopping list.

Helmet

It is a legal requirement that you wear a helmet in races, so it's just as well to practice it in training. You don't need a top-of-the-range aerodynamic cone-shaped helmet — in fact a more basic model, with plenty of air vents, will keep your head cooler. Make sure that the helmet you buy is the correct size and adjust the straps and casing for a snug fit. It should not move about from side to side or back to front when you move your head, even before you have done up the strap.

Pedals and shoes

If you're going to ride your bike in running shoes, then simple platform pedals are fine. If you intend to use a clipless pedal system, such as Look or Shimano, then you'll need compatible bike shoes. Bike shoes attach to the pedals using cleats, and it's important that these cleats are positioned correctly to maximize efficiency and avoid possible injury problems.

Most clipless pedals have a tension spring, which you can adjust to make it easier or harder to release your foot. If you're new to being "attached" to your bike, it's a good idea to set them on the easiest release position.

Bike shoes are very stiff-soled, made of fiberglass or carbon fiber. This offers good power transfer, but it also makes them extremely difficult to walk in and slippery, which is why many triathletes who do opt for clipless pedals begin and end their race with the shoes attached to the pedals. Tri shoes often have drain holes to help get rid of excess water post-swim. They also have a single-strap Velcro fastening across the top to make them easier to get on and off. The strap opens to the outside of the foot, not the inside, to keep it away from the chain when you're slipping on your shoes, on the move (see Resources, page 172).

Tri bars

Clip-on tri bars (or aero bars) enable you to achieve a flatter body position and ride faster, but they take a bit of getting used to. Get advice from a good bike shop to make sure the set you choose is compatible with your bike frame, comfortable and adjustable.

HOT TIP
Put your name, address and contact number in your helmet in case of an accident.

Cycle clothing

The three factors to think about here are comfort, temperature control and safety. Cycle shorts or tights, with internal padding, are a must for comfort. Remember to "go commando" — the whole point of the cushioned gusset is to reduce chafing!

Don't wear loose clothing that flaps around — this will create additional resistance and slow you down. For tops and jackets, opt for breathable, wicking fabrics and dress in layers so that you can adjust your temperature. Long-sleeved tops guard against road rash if you have a fall, while bright colors and reflective panels make you more visible to other road users. Rear pockets are useful for carrying fuel and spares. Cycle gloves take the pressure off your hands and also protect them in the event of a fall.

Eyewear

Eye protection is important, given that you're going to be spending a lot of time training in the great outdoors, exposed to harmful UV rays. Choose glasses that are sports specific, not fashion models. Sport sunglasses are designed to stay on even when you are moving around a lot and usually have a wraparound style and a sweat-resistance nose bridge to prevent slippage. Lenses should be polycarbonate, which offers 100 percent UV protection and is shatterproof. Polarized lenses don't give much depth and so holes won't show up in the road surface or uneven terrain. It's not necessary to have different pairs of sunglasses for cycling and running.

Spares and tools

Even if you don't intend to do anything more technical than raise your saddle, you need a few basic tools — a multipurpose bike tool, spare inner tubes, a set of tire levers, a pump, chain lube, and lights, at the minimum. Learning to fix a flat fast might save the day if you get a puncture during a race or invest in a canister of latex foam sealant, which mends the puncture and reinflates the tire, enabling you to continue cycling without even having to take the tire off. It won't give you the tire pressure you'd get with a pump but it will certainly get you through the end of the bike leg and stop you from having to drop out. And if you're really clueless about bike maintenance, be sure to make friends with your local bike store!

SPORTS BRAS

Whether you are an AA or an FF cup, there is a sports bra out there for you. In general, "encapsulated" bras, which separate and support each breast in its own cup (sometimes with underwiring for extra support) are best for bigger-breasted women, while "compression" bras (which press the breasts against the rib cage to reduce movement) work better for the flatter-chested. Try lots of bras on and jog around in them to see how supportive they feel. The bra should be snug, but not so tight that it restricts your breathing and it should stay level all the way round, rather than riding up at the back. Make sure the straps are wide enough to give proper support and not dig into your skin and soft enough not to rub. They should also be adjustable, as the fabric will stretch over time and you'll need to shorten them. Technical fabrics (as opposed to cotton) wick away sweat so that your body stays dry and comfortable and you avoid chafing — flat-stitched seams also help. See Resources, page 172, for details.

Running gear

Running is the simplest of the three disciplines when it comes to getting outfitted. All you really need is a decent pair of running shoes and, if you're a woman, a sports bra. You can run in any comfortable clothing, though technical fabrics are better for breathability, keeping you cool and dry. Cycle tops and jackets are fine for running, although I don't advise running in bike shorts (though tri shorts are OK, see page 112). Again, a layering system works best for controlling temperature.

As for shoes, there are running shoes out there for all shapes, sizes, foot-strike patterns and budgets. The choice can be overwhelming, so the best solution is to visit a specialized running or triathlon store, where knowledgeable staff can offer advice and gait analysis (see Resources, page 172).

SEVEN TIPS FOR BUYING RUNNING SHOES

1. Buy designated running shoes. Cross-trainers, tennis shoes and fashion sneakers are not suitable for running!

2. Shop for running shoes in the afternoon or even better, after a run, when your feet are slightly bigger.

3. Try both shoes on together and stand, don't sit, when assessing the amount of space in the front of the shoe. You need approximately 1/2 inch beyond your longest toe (which is not always the big toe).

4. If you wear orthotics, take them with you when you buy running shoes. Try the shoes on without socks if that's how you intend to wear them and remember that shoes without seams and ridges inside and integrated tongues reduce the chafing factor. If you run in socks, wear the socks you are going to train in.

5. Expect instant comfort. Running shoes shouldn't need to be broken in. Many stores now offer treadmills to test out running shoes. If not, at least run a few steps in the shoes, either around or outside the store.

6. Bear in mind that you might need different shoes for training than you need for racing, depending on the distance you'll be covering and/or surfaces you'll be running on.

7. Expect running shoes to last 275 to 500 miles or approximately six months.

Training tools

Gone are the days when a wristwatch, perhaps with a lap counter and timer, constituted a training tool. These days, you can monitor your heart rate, track your pace and energy expenditure, and measure your distance and global position via satellite, all at the touch of a button. Meanwhile, bike-mounted gizmos enable you not only to see your pace and mileage, but also to monitor cadence and assess power output. None of this gadgetry is essential, of course, but it can aid your understanding of how your body is responding to training and can be very addictive! (See Resources, page 172.)

GPS

Global positioning systems (GPS) are the ultimate in performance monitoring and, with wristwatch-size versions now available, no longer necessitate carrying a brick-sized unit on your upper arm. GPS tracks your location, wherever you are in the world, enabling you to check your pace and distance while you are on the move, as well as elevation and calorie expenditure. You can also download your route and session data onto your PC afterward (some models even allow you to do this wirelessly), giving you the option of comparing and contrasting your performances and even measuring yourself against other users. The latest systems also incorporate heart rate monitoring and bike cadence (though you sometimes have to fork out extra for the relevant bits and pieces), so you have everything you could possibly need in one package.

Heart rate monitors

For a simpler gadget, you can't beat a heart rate monitor. The chest strap sends information about your heart rate to the wristwatch, so you get unbiased feedback while you exercise as well as being able to check your average heart rate during the session afterward. Heart rate monitors vary in function and price. Most models enable you to set the upper and lower boundaries of your exercise intensity, allow you to enter personal data, and calculate calories and fat percentage burned. Higher-end options allow you to download data onto your computer or track your distance and speed via a footpod (a cheaper but less accurate alternative to GPS). Only pay for functions you think you'll use and make sure the watch face is clearly readable and the buttons easy to press on the move.

Bike computers and cadence monitors

For cycling, the most useful gadget is a bike computer, essentially a wristwatch that attaches to your handlebars. A basic bike computer measures speed and distance via a small magnet attached to a wheel spoke and a sensor attached to the front fork or rear stay (if using a turbo trainer, the speed sensor and magnet need to be located on the rear wheel). Some computers come complete with a cadence monitor, which operates via another magnet attached to your pedal crank and a sensor located adjacently on the frame. If you get really geeky, other functions include gradient monitors to record your inclines, altimeters to measure altitude change and power sensors, which measure chain speed and tension to provide feedback on cycling efficiency and left/right leg balance. All this data is transmitted and displayed on the handlebar-mounted display, either via wires or wirelessly and it can be downloaded to your PC.

Drink bottles and hydration packs

For longer runs and bike rides, a hydration pack (a backpack with a bladder inside, which you access via a long straw) can be useful. Alternatively, a handheld water bottle or hydration belt, filled with small bottles or gels, enables you to carry fluid on the run. Attach two drink bottle cages to your bike so that you can carry plenty of fluid.

VOICE OF EXPERIENCE: RICHARD ALLEN

You don't need to spend thousands of dollars on equipment — you just have to make sure it fits properly and works well. The fit is particularly important with wetsuits, goggles and shoes and, of course, your bike. A cheap wetsuit that fits well is far better than the very best wetsuit that does not fit you properly. When you buy new gear, it's worth keeping your old version as a spare, just in case something breaks. At least you know it works.

Turbo trainer

This simple device turns your bike into a stationary cycle. The back wheel is clamped to the steel-framed trainer using a quick-release skewer and you ride as normal, with the rear wheel being resisted by the turbo's roller, usually via magnetic resistance or a fluid-filled system. Some turbo trainers have handlebar-mounted controls, which allow you to change the resistance against the rear wheel; others require you to get off to adjust the resistance, though you can use your gears to upshift or downshift. Look for a model that is quiet, sturdy and easy to assemble. Some fold flat for easier storage.

Most turbos leave the front wheel of the bike lower than the back — if this isn't adjustable, you can put a book under the front wheel to lift it up level. I find the Yellow Pages work great or you can buy a designated wheel block.

Race gear

And finally, here are a few pieces of gear that may help you on the day.

Tri suits

This is a one- or two-piece outfit, designed to be worn throughout the race. You wear it under your wetsuit for the swim (or in place of a swimsuit in a pool swim), then cycle and run in it. This saves you from wasting time in transition.

HOT TIP

Use your turbo beside a mirror so you can check your position and adjust if necessary.

Get the right fit and a tri suit won't chafe or rub and the fast-drying, breathable fabric ensures that you don't end up drenched in sweat once you start moving on dry land. A tri suit also offers some padding in the gusset for the bike ride, but not so much that it will restrict your running.

Tri suits are a good bet for sprint and Olympic distance races, although for longer distance events when you're out on the road for hours, you may need warmer gear and more seat padding for the bike ride. Many tri suits also have strategically placed pockets in which you can stash your race nutrition or bike spares.

The suit should feel snug, but not so tight that it's bisecting you! Look for flatlock seams or seam-free suits and rubber grips on the leg hems to stop them from riding up. A one-piece suit is more streamlined than a two-piece and the lack of waistband means less risk of chafing, but it can be a pain to take off to go to the bathroom and many women's one pieces lack built-in bra support — so women may need to wear a sports bra underneath.

Race belt

Mount your race number on this elastic belt and you don't have to mess around putting paper numbers on your back (for the bike) and front (for the run). You simply twist it around between the two disciplines. You can even wear your race belt underneath your wetsuit during the swim.

Elastic laces

Many triathletes swap their usual laces for elastic ones in races. These allow you to get your feet in your shoes without having to loosen the laces or tie them up, saving time in transition.

COMPRESSION CLOTHING

Compression clothing is quite the thing in triathlon these days. The myriad benefits it offers, according to the hype, are improved blood flow, reduced muscle oscillation (causing less muscle damage), warmth and better recovery. But what does the research say? Well, it's surprisingly positive. Which is probably why the British Triathlon Federation has decked out all its pro triathletes in the stuff.

A study published in the *Journal of Sports Science* reported a 27 percent reduction in impact force when custom-fit compression shorts were worn, while recent research reported lower energy expenditure among distance runners wearing compression tights compared to normal running tights. However, according to research in the *Canadian Journal of Sport Science*, the pressure exerted by a compression garment must be graduated in order to mimic the hemodynamic (blood flow) effect of exercise and to increase venous return. In other words, the compression should be greatest at the bottom and exert less pressure farther up. 2XU and Skins all offer this graded compression (see Resources, page 172, for details).

CHAPTER SEVEN THE TRAINING

So you've read the theory, bought the gear, earmarked your race and you're raring to get started! This is the point at which many books and magazines introduce you to the theory of periodization. It's one of those triathlon favorites — partly, I suspect, because triathlon is a seasonal sport — lending itself very well to the concept.

Periodization is about dividing up the year or other training period into blocks called cycles, which have a specific focus that relates to the time of year — off-season, preseason, competition, for example. Each phase is divided into smaller meso- and micro- cycles, which, again, have a specific focus. Periodization is all very well, but it makes the assumption that you intend to live like an athlete, allowing your year to be shaped by your sport and competing in races throughout the season. This can be quite a daunting prospect if you just fancy trying a triathlon or two — and it isn't a prerequisite for success.

Just to be clear, I'm not saying that your training shouldn't follow a logical, progressive path — just that you don't have to periodize your whole year or season to enjoy the sport of triathlon. What is important, however, is that your training regime has three key attributes: structure, progression and consistency.

Structuring a successful training program

Getting on your bike and riding with no specific aim or purpose isn't training, it's cycling. Each and every session you do should be a stepping stone on your journey toward your goal — whether it's improving your general fitness or your discipline-specific skill and technique. This is because training (when it's done correctly) causes the body to adapt to the challenges you place upon it, rather than saying, "Stop! Where's the couch? I can't cope with this!"

These adaptations take place in practically every system in the body. For example, the heart gets stronger, enabling it to pump more blood out with every beat. Nerve to muscle communication improves, so that you can execute movements more efficiently and powerfully. Connective tissues, like tendons and ligaments, grow hardier and more injury-resistant and the body becomes more proficient at using fat as a source of fuel, which not only helps shrink your waistline, but also conserves its precious stores of carbohydrate. All of these changes will enable you to bike, swim and run faster, stronger and longer. But to benefit, you have to get the training formula right. And that's where the FITT acronym comes in handy.

The FITT Factors

FITT stands for Frequency, Intensity, Time and Type.

Frequency: How often am I going to train?
Intensity: How hard am I going to train?
Time: How long am I going to train for?
Type: What type of training am I going to do?

The strengths and weaknesses you identified and goals you set back in Chapter One should help you answer these questions. For example, do you need to improve your feel for the water by swimming more often? Do you need to substitute some flat runs for hillier ones? Or spend longer in the saddle?

Starter's orders

If you are a novice exerciser, it's particularly important to establish a good base of aerobic fitness before you start to work your way up to more challenging sessions. It's also sensible to spend some time honing your technique — there is little point in working harder and faster if you don't have the necessary skill to run, cycle and swim without putting yourself at risk of injury.

What's more, while the tougher, faster sessions are essential for maximizing your fitness gains, you need to take a little and often approach to them. Most triathlon training programs dedicate only 20–30 percent of overall training time to sessions performed at anaerobic intensity. Much more than that is just too taxing on the body.

Once you've set out your own personal plan (or opted for one of the programs on

pages 120–125), be consistent with your training. If you train sporadically, your poor old body doesn't know whether it needs to make those fitness adaptations or not and the chances are it won't bother!

That's not to say you can never take a day's rest. In fact, while you'd be right to think that it's the training that facilitates your fitness gains, it's actually during rest that the body makes the necessary changes. Essentially, training breaks down the body and rest builds it up. If you train too hard, too long or too often, you won't give your body sufficient recovery time, and you won't progress at an optimal rate. There is no hard and fast rule about how much rest you need, but in general, it's advisable to take at least one full day off per week. It's also important to spread out your harder sessions through the week rather than doing them back to back.

As your fitness improves, you need to increase the level of challenge in order to keep making progress. Once the body has become too comfortable with any given training regime, it no longer provides the necessary stimulus to trigger adaptations.

But don't try to change all the FITT variables at once. It's not wise to increase both the duration and intensity of a session — focus on one or the other. Similarly, don't increase the frequency of your training as well as the length of your sessions.

HOT TIP
Consider entering single discipline events in your build-up to the race, such as 3.1 mile (5 km) runs or sportives — long-distance cycling events.

TEN GOLDEN RULES OF SUCCESSFUL TRAINING

1. If you are new to triathlon, start by building a good aerobic base through steady-paced sessions in all three disciplines.
2. Once you've built a good base of stamina, introduce some more intense sessions, such as intervals, hills and time trials.
3. Don't neglect skills practice — fitness is important, but it's only part of the equation.
4. Keep a training diary to record your progress and help you stay motivated.
5. Go for frequency rather than longer training time in the disciplines that you're learning the basics of; this will help to lay down the correct motor skills and neuromuscular pathways.
6. Spend a good proportion of your allotted training time on the discipline you are least comfortable with.
7. Keep up the training in your strongest discipline so you don't lose ground.
8. Aim to cover race distance plus a half in training. This gives you confidence as well as the requisite fitness.
9. Support your training in the three sports with regular core stability, strength and flexibility work.
10. As the race draws nearer, gear your training more specifically to its demands. For example, practicing open-water skills for an open-water race or hillier rides for an undulating bike leg.

On your marks

The training programs that begin on page 120 come courtesy of triathlon coach Richard Allen, who, as a former winner of the London Triathlon, should know a thing or two! The two beginner programs (one for sprint, one for Olympic distance) assume that you already have a base level of fitness and can swim, cycle and run reasonably well. The improvers' schedule is aimed at those who have a triathlon or two under their belt. There are two sessions per week in each sport. It's up to you to fit them into your schedule as best suits you, but don't perform the higher intensity sessions (session 2 in each sport) on consecutive days. That said, no program is set in stone. Listen to your body and adapt your training where necessary. Richard also has this advice:

*   Don't skip the warm-ups and cool-downs.
*   Schedule in rest days once or twice a week.
*   Take an easy week (doing just a couple of easy-paced sessions) halfway through the program if you feel you need to.
*   Do not train right up to your race. Allow an easier week to taper and recover before the event. Read more about the countdown to race day in Chapter Eight.
*   If you lack confidence or stamina in swimming, use fins for the main sets to begin with.
*   If you have to skip sessions due to time constraints, don't miss the aerobic ones (session 1 in the programs) — these are the mainstay of your training.

- Every two weeks, do one of your steady run sessions straight off the bike, with a practice transition. Alternatively, do a 1/2 mile or 5 minute run after all your outdoor rides.

- To see how you're progressing, substitute a hard-paced session with a time trial in your chosen discipline. Only do this once per discipline during the six-week period.

KEY TO EFFORT LEVELS

The key below gives you an idea of how each effort level described in the programs overleaf should feel, with a corresponding RPE and heart rate range (work out your personal heart rate range below).

Easy: You should feel as if you could go on all day! Effort level: less than 60 percent or 4–5 out of 10.

Steady: This should be a comfortable pace at which you can still hold a conversation (well, unless you're swimming, that is!). For most people, this will be slower than race pace.
Effort level: 60–75 percent or 6–7 out of 10.

Tempo: You should be breathing hard and won't feel like wasting energy chatting. This equates most closely to the pace at which you'll be racing.
Effort level: 75–85 percent or 7–8 out of 10.

Hard: This should be the hardest pace you can sustain for the given duration. Close to an all-out effort.
Effort level: 85–95 percent or 8–9 out of 10.

WORKING OUT YOUR HEART RATE

The "220 minus your age" formula is commonly used to get an estimated maximum heart rate value, but used on its own, can be as much as 20 beats out. The Karvonen Formula takes your resting heart rate into account (the number of times your heart beats per minute at complete rest) — and offers a more accurate way of determining your heart rate range at any given effort level.

To use the Karvonen Formula, you need to know your resting heart rate (ideally recorded first thing in the morning before food or caffeine) and your age-determined or actual, maximum heart rate, which can be measured in a VO_2 max test at a laboratory.

Example: You are forty years old. Your resting heart rate (RHR) is 70 bpm, your age-predicted maximum heart rate (MHR) is 180 and the training program tells you to work at 75–85 percent of your maximum.

Let's start by working out what your heart rate would be at 75 percent effort:

$75\% = (MHR - RHR) \times 75\% + RHR$

$75\% = (180 - 70) \times 75\% + 70$

$75\% = (110) \times 75\% = 82.5 + 70$

$75\% = 152.5$ bpm

Now let's substitute 75 for 85 percent effort, to get the heart rate range:

$85\% = (MHR - RHR) \times 85\% + RHR$

$85\% = (180 - 70) \times 85\% + 70$

$85\% = (110) \times 85\% = 93.5 + 70$

$85\% = 163.5$ bpm

In this example, the heart rate range for working at 75–85 per effort would be 152–163 bpm.

BEGINNER'S SPRINT-DISTANCE 6-WEEK PROGRAM

	SWIM TRAINING	BIKE TRAINING	RUN TRAINING
WEEK 1	**SESSION 1** Warm-up: 6x50 meters easy with 15-sec rests. Include some drills. Main set: 200/100/200 meters steady with 25-sec rests Cool-down: 100 meters easy	1 hour steady road ride	30 mins steady road/trail run
	SESSION 2 Warm-up: 12x25 meters easy with 15-sec rests. Include some drills. Main set: 12x25 meters tempo with 10-sec rests Cool-down: 2x25 meters kick, 50 meters pull buoy easy with 15-sec rests	Stationary bike/turbo trainer Warm-up: 5 mins easy, 5 mins steady. Main set: 5x (2 mins hard, 1 min easy) Cool-down: 5 mins easy	Treadmill/road run Warm-up: 5 mins easy, 5 mins steady. Main set: 2x (5 mins tempo, 2 mins easy) Cool-down: 5 mins easy.
WEEK 2	**SESSION 1** Warm-up: 6x50 meters easy with 15-sec rests. Include some drills. Main set: 4x50 meters/1x100 meters/4x50 meters steady with 20-sec rests Cool-down:100 meters easy	1 hour steady road ride	20 mins steady road/trail run
	SESSION 2 Warm-up: 12x25 meters easy with 15-sec rests. Include some drills. Main set: 6x100 meters tempo with 20-sec rests Cool-down: 2x25 meters kick, 50 meters pull buoy easy with 15-sec rests	Stationary bike/turbo trainer Warm-up: 5 mins easy, 5 mins steady. Main set: 3x (5 mins tempo, 2 mins easy) Cool-down: 5 mins easy	Treadmill/road run Warm-up: 5 mins easy, 5 mins steady. Main set: 5x (1 min hard, 1 min easy) Cool-down: 5 mins easy.
WEEK 3	**SESSION 1** Warm-up: 6x50 meters easy with 15-sec rests. Include some drills. Main set: 5x100 meters steady with 20-sec rests Cool-down: 100 meters easy	1 hour steady road ride	40 mins steady road/trail run
	SESSION 2 Warm-up: 12x25 meters easy with 15-sec rests. Include some drills. Main set: 8x50 meters hard pace with 15-sec rests Cool-down: 2 x25 meters kick, 50 meters pull buoy easy with 15-sec rests	Stationary bike/turbo trainer Warm-up: 5 mins easy, 5 mins steady. Main set: 5x (3 mins hard, 1 min easy) Cool-down: 5 mins easy	Treadmill/road run Warm-up: 5 mins easy, 5 mins steady. Main set: 3x (5 mins tempo, 2 mins easy) Cool-down: 5 mins easy.

	SWIM TRAINING	BIKE TRAINING	RUN TRAINING
WEEK 4	**SESSION 1** Warm-up: 6x50 meters easy with 15-sec rests. Include some drills. Main set: 6x50 meters/1x150 meters/6x50 meters steady with 20-sec rests Cool-down: 100 meters easy	75 mins steady road ride	20 mins steady road/trail run
	SESSION 2 Warm-up: 12x25 meters easy with 15-sec rests. Include some drills. Main set: 8x50 meters hard pace with 15-sec rests Cool-down: 2 x25 meters kick, 50 meters pull buoy easy with 15-sec rests	Stationary bike/turbo trainer Warm-up: 5 mins easy, 5 mins steady. Main set: 4x (5 mins tempo, 2 mins easy) Cool-down: 5 mins easy	Treadmill/road run Warm-up: 5 mins easy, 5 mins steady Main set: 5x (2 mins hard, 1 min easy) Cool-down: 5 mins easy
WEEK 5	**SESSION 1** Warm-up: 6x50m easy with 15-sec rests. Include some drills. Main set: 4x50 meters/1x100 meters/1x200 meters steady with 20-sec rests Cool-down: 100 meters easy	1 hour steady road ride	50 mins steady road/trail run
	SESSION 2 Warm-up: 12x25 meters easy with 15-sec rests. Include some drills and short sprints. Main set: 20x25 meters hard pace with 10-sec rests Cool-down: 2 x25 meters kick, 50 meters pull buoy easy with 15-sec rests	Stationary bike/turbo trainer Warm-up: 5 mins easy, 5 mins steady. Main set: 5x (4 mins hard, 1 min easy) Cool-down: 5 mins easy	Treadmill/road run Warm-up: 5 mins easy, 5 mins steady Main set: 4x (5 mins tempo, 2 mins easy) Cool-down: 5 mins easy
WEEK 6	**SESSION 1** Warm-up: 6x50 meters easy with 15-sec rests. Include some drills. Main set: 10x100 meters steady with 20-sec rests Cool-down: 100 meters easy	90 mins steady road ride	20 mins steady road/trail run
	SESSION 2 Warm-up: 12x25 meters easy with 15-sec rests. Include some drills and short sprints. Main set: 8x100 meters tempo with 20-sec rests Cool-down: 2 x25 meters kick, 50 meters pull buoy easy with 15-sec rests	Stationary bike/turbo trainer Warm-up: 5 mins easy, 5 mins steady. Main set: 5x (5 mins tempo, 2 mins easy) Cool-down: 5 mins easy	Treadmill/road run Warm-up: 5 mins easy, 5 mins steady Main set: 5x (3 mins hard, 1 min easy) Cool-down: 5 mins easy

BEGINNER'S OLYMPIC-DISTANCE 6-WEEK PROGRAM

	SWIM TRAINING	BIKE TRAINING	RUN TRAINING
WEEK 1	**SESSION 1** Warm-up: 6x100 meters easy with 15-sec rests. Include some drills. Main set: 3x50 meters/1x100 meters/1x200 meters/1x300 meters steady with 25-sec rests Cool-down: 100 meters easy	90 mins steady road ride	45 mins steady road/trail run
	SESSION 2 Warm-up: 12x50 meters easy with 15-sec rests. Include some drills. Main set: 10x50 meters hard pace with 20-sec rests Cool-down: 2x25 meters kick, 50 meters pull buoy easy with 15-sec rests	Stationary bike/turbo trainer Warm-up: 5 mins easy, 5 mins steady. Main set: 5x (3 mins hard, 1 min easy) Cool-down: 5 mins easy	Treadmill/road run Warm-up: 5 mins easy, 5 mins steady Main set: 4x (5 mins tempo, 2 mins easy) Cool-down: 5 mins easy
WEEK 2	**SESSION 1** Warm-up: 6x100 meters easy with 15-sec rests. Include some drills. Main set: 3x50 meters/4x100 meters/4x50 meters steady with 15-sec rests Cool-down: 100 meters easy	90 mins steady road ride	30 mins steady road/trail run
	SESSION 2 Warm-up: 12x50 meters easy with 15-sec rests. Include some drills and build pace. Main set: 8x100 meters tempo with 20-sec rests Cool-down: 2x25 meters kick, 50m pull buoy easy with 15-sec rests	Stationary bike/turbo trainer Warm-up: 5 mins easy, 5 mins steady Main set: 5x (5 mins tempo, 2 mins easy) Cool-down: 5 mins easy	Treadmill/road run Warm-up: 5 mins easy, 5 mins steady Main set: 5x (2 mins hard, 1 min easy) Cool-down: 5 mins easy
WEEK 3	**SESSION 1** Warm-up: 6x100 meters easy with 15-sec rests. Include some drills. Main set: 5x50 meters/5x100 meters steady with 15-sec rests Cool-down: 100 meters easy	90 mins steady road ride	40 mins steady road/trail run
	SESSION 2 Warm-up: 12x50 meters easy with 15-sec rests. Include some drills and short sprints. Main set: 12x50 meters hard pace with 15-sec rests Cool-down: 2x25 meters kick, 50m pull buoy easy with 15-sec rests	Stationary bike/turbo trainer Warm-up: 5 mins easy, 5 mins steady Main set: 5x (4 mins hard, 1 min easy) Cool-down: 5 mins easy	Treadmill/road run Warm-up: 5 mins easy, 5 mins steady Main set: 5x (5 mins tempo, 2 mins easy) Cool-down: 5 mins easy

	SWIM TRAINING	BIKE TRAINING	RUN TRAINING
WEEK 4	**SESSION 1** Warm-up: 6x100 meters easy with 15-sec rests. Include some drills. Main set: 4x50 meters/4x100 meters/2x200 meters/2x50 meters steady with 20-sec rests Cool-down: 100 meters easy	1 hour 50 mins steady road ride	30 mins steady road/trail run
	SESSION 2 Warm-up: 12x50 meters easy with 15-sec rests. Include some drills and build pace. Main set: 10x100 meters tempo pace with 20-sec rests Cool-down: 2 x25 meters kick, 50 meters pull buoy easy with 15-sec rests	Stationary bike/turbo trainer Warm-up: 5 mins easy, 5 mins steady Main set: 6x (5 mins tempo, 2 mins easy) Cool-down: 5 mins easy	Treadmill/road run Warm-up: 5 mins easy, 5 mins steady Main set: 5x (3 mins hard, 1 min easy) Cool-down: 5 mins easy
WEEK 5	**SESSION 1** Warm-up: 6x100 meters easy with 15-sec rests. Include some drills. Main set: 200 meters/5x50 meters/300 meters steady with 30-sec rests Cool-down: 100 meters easy	90 mins steady road ride	50 mins steady road/trail run
	SESSION 2 Warm-up: 12x50 meters easy with 15-sec rests. Include some drills and short sprints. Main set: 15x50 meters hard pace with 15-sec rests Cool-down: 2x25 meters kick, 50m pull buoy easy with 15-sec rests	Stationary bike/turbo trainer Warm-up: 5 mins easy, 5 mins steady Main set: 5x (5 mins hard, 2 mins easy) Cool-down: 5 mins easy	Treadmill/road run Warm-up: 5 mins easy, 5 mins steady Main set: 6x (5 mins tempo, 2 mins easy) Cool-down: 5 mins easy
WEEK 6	**SESSION 1** Warm-up: 6x100 meters easy with 15-sec rests. Include some drills. Main set: 15x100 meters steady with 20-sec rests Cool-down: 100 meters easy	2 hours 15 mins steady road ride	30 mins steady road/trail run
	SESSION 2 Warm-up: 12x50 meters easy with 15-sec rests. Include some drills and short sprints. Main set: 12x100 meters tempo with 20-sec rests Cool-down: 2x25 meters kick, 50m pull buoy easy with 15-sec rests	Stationary bike/turbo trainer Warm-up: 5 mins easy, 5 mins steady Main set: 7x (5 mins tempo, 2 mins easy) Cool-down: 5 mins easy	Treadmill/road run Warm-up: 5 mins easy, 5 mins steady Main set: 5x (4 mins hard, 1 min easy) Cool-down: 5 mins easy

IMPROVER'S OLYMPIC-DISTANCE 6-WEEK PROGRAM

	SWIM TRAINING	BIKE TRAINING	RUN TRAINING
WEEK 1	**SESSION 1** Warm-up: 5x200 meters easy with 15-sec rests. Include some drills. Main set: 100 meters/200 meters/300 meters/400 meters steady with 30-sec rests Cool-down: 100 meters easy	2 hour steady road ride	1 hour steady road/trail run
	SESSION 2 Warm-up: 10x100 meters easy with 15-sec rests. Include some drills and sprints. Main set: 12x 50 meters hard with 10 secs rest Cool-down: 2x25 meters kick, 50m pull buoy easy with 15 secs rest	Stationary bike/turbo trainer Warm up: 5 mins easy, 5 mins steady Main set: 5x (4 mins hard, 1 min easy) Cool-down: 5 mins easy	Treadmill/road run Warm up: 5 mins easy, 5 mins steady Main set: 6x (5 mins tempo, 2 mins easy) Cool-down: 5 mins easy
WEEK 2	**SESSION 1** Warm up: 5x200 meters easy with 15-sec rests. Include some drills. Main set: 4x50 meters/5x100 meters/6x50 meters steady with 15-sec rests Cool-down: 100 meters easy	2 hour steady road ride	40 mins steady road/trail run
	SESSION 2 Warm up: 10x100 meters easy with 15-sec rests. Include some drills and build pace. Main set: 12x100 meters tempo with 15-sec rests Cool-down: 2x25 meters kick, 50m pull buoy easy with 15-sec rests	Stationary bike/turbo trainer Warm up: 5 mins easy, 5 mins steady Main set: 7x (5 mins tempo, 2 mins easy) Cool-down: 5 mins easy	Treadmill/road run Warm up: 5 mins easy, 5 mins steady Main set: 5 x (3 mins hard, 1 min easy) Cool-down: 5 mins easy
WEEK 3	**SESSION 1** Warm up: 5x200 meters easy with 15-sec rests. Include some drills. Main set: 4x50 meters/2x100 meters/1x200 meters/2x100 meters/ 4x50 meters steady with 15-sec rests Cool-down: 100 meters easy	2 hour steady road ride	75 mins steady road/trail run
	SESSION 2 Warm up: 10x100 meters easy with 15-sec rests. Include some drills and short sprints. Main set: 16x50 meters hard with 10-sec rests Cool-down: 2x25 meters kick, 50m pull buoy easy with 15-sec rests	Stationary bike/turbo trainer Warm up: 5 mins easy, 5 mins steady Main set: 5x (5 mins hard, 2 mins easy) Cool-down: 5 mins easy	Treadmill/road run Warm up: 5 mins easy, 5 mins steady Main set: 5x (7 mins tempo, 2 mins easy) Cool-down: 5 mins easy

	SWIM TRAINING	BIKE TRAINING	RUN TRAINING
WEEK 4	**SESSION 1** Warm up: 5x200 meters easy with 15-sec rests. Include some drills. Main set: 2x50 meters/2x100 meters/2x200 meters/2x300 meters/4x50 meters steady with 30-sec rests Cool-down: 100 meters easy	2 hour 30 min steady road ride	40 mins steady road/trail run
	SESSION 2 Warm up: 10x100 meters easy with 15-sec rests. Include some drills and build pace. Main set: 14x100 meters tempo with 15-sec rests Cool-down: 2x25 meters kick, 50 meters pull buoy easy with 15-sec rests	Stationary bike/turbo trainer Warm up: 5 mins easy, 5 mins steady Main set: 2x (6 mins tempo, 2 mins easy), 2x (7 mins tempo, 2 mins easy) Cool-down: 5 mins easy	Treadmill/road run Warm up: 5 mins easy, 5 mins steady Main set: 5x (4 mins hard, 1 min easy) Cool-down: 5 mins easy
WEEK 5	**SESSION 1** Warm up: 5x200 meters easy with 15-sec rests. Include some drills. Main set: 5x200 meters steady with 25-sec rests Cool-down: 100 meters easy	2 hour steady road ride	90 mins steady road/trail run
	SESSION 2 Warm up: 10x100 meters easy with 15-sec rests. Include some drills and short sprints. Main set: 10x100 meters hard with 15-sec rests Cool-down: 2x25 meters kick, 50 meters pull buoy easy with 15-sec rests	Stationary bike/turbo trainer Warm up: 5 mins easy, 5 mins steady Main set: 6x (5 mins hard, 2 mins easy) Cool-down: 5 mins easy	Treadmill/road run Warm up: 5 mins easy, 5 mins steady Main set: 4x (10 mins tempo, 2 mins easy) Cool-down: 5 mins easy
WEEK 6	**SESSION 1** Warm up: 5x200 meters easy with 15-sec rests. Include some drills. Main set: 4x100 meters/2 x 200 meters/400 meters/2x200 meters/ 4x100 meters steady with 25-sec rests	3 hour steady road ride	40 min steady road/trail run
	SESSION 2 Warm up: 10x100 meters easy with 15-sec rests. Include some drills and build pace. Main set: 16x100 meters tempo with 15-sec rests Cool-down: 2x25 meters kick, 50 meters pull buoy easy with 15-sec rests	Stationary bike/turbo trainer Warm up: 5 mins easy, 5 mins steady Main set: 5 mins tempo, 2 mins easy, 10 mins tempo, 2 mins easy, 15 mins tempo, 3 mins easy, 10 mins tempo, 2 mins easy, 5 mins tempo Cool-down: 10 mins easy	Treadmill/road run Warm up: 5 mins easy, 5 mins steady Main set: 5x (5 mins hard, 2 mins easy) Cool-down: 5 mins easy

VOICE OF
EXPERIENCE:
RICHARD ALLEN

If you really want to make
sure that every session
counts, it's worth hiring a
triathlon coach. You can opt
for face-to-face coaching
or e-mail or phone-based
services. Going on personal
recommendation or using
a coach affiliated with a
big event ensures they will
be reputable. Or search
triathlon federation Web
sites to find an appropriately
qualified coach in your
area. But remember,
experience counts as much
as qualifications and you
need to make sure that you
get along with, trust and
like the person who will
be telling you what to do!

SEVEN WAYS TO FIT IN YOUR TRAINING

Cycle to work or to the station

If the journey is too long to make twice in one day, you could leave your bike at work and cycle it back later in the week. This will also help fine-tune your bike handling skills.

Train at lunchtime

A lunchtime run or swim won't make inroads into your day and won't have such an impact on your home and social life.

Run to and from work

You can make the morning session a challenging one and the evening session a recovery run or vice versa — but don't do this every day or you risk overdoing things.

Use the gym

You can combine a run and bike session by using the treadmill and exercise bike at the gym, without having to get changed and organized for two sports.

Invest in a turbo trainer

A turbo trainer enables you to get a ride in while you watch TV or chat with your partner. It also makes short sessions worthwhile, whereas if you only have 30 minutes to spare you might not bother getting geared up for an outdoor ride.

Join a club

Coached sessions at set times can help you schedule your training. Clubs differ in terms of what they offer, but most have coached sessions in all three disciplines, enabling you to improve on your weaknesses and play on your strengths. You also get great support, sociability and motivation. See Resources on page 172 for details.

Race more!

Races are the perfect way to train for races! Prioritize the ones that are important to you and use the others as training and rehearsal. You can focus on one specific discipline or transition, in your build-up races.

CAMPING IT UP

A triathlon training camp is the ultimate way to combine your training with some sun and fun. You have the luxury of expert coaching, technical support and great camaraderie — with no demands on your time other than training, eating and sleeping. You don't have to be a budding Tim Don to benefit, either. In fact, when I went on my first training camp, I barely knew what order you did the three sports in and had never taken part in a race. Ask club friends and use the Internet and magazines to get a feel for what different camps offer. Some are more serious than others — for example, one might be targeted toward training for long-distance events such as Ironman, while others are more geared toward novices. See Resources, page 172, for more details.

CHAPTER EIGHT **THE RACING**

Ready to put your newfound skills and fitness to the test? Then it's time to start thinking about races. This chapter takes you through the whole process, from picking the right events to making sure everything goes smoothly on the big day.

Choosing races

Whether it's your debut race or you are planning a whole season of triathlon challenges, it is worth doing a little research prior to signing up for events. In the US, the number of races is multiplying each year, so how do you narrow down the choice?

Distance is an obvious factor to consider — if you're new to triathlon, it's advisable to start off with a sprint or supersprint event to get a feel for the sport without overwhelming yourself. (See Chapter One for a reminder of the standard race distances.) Some coaches recommend picking a debut race with a pool swim, but my personal choice was a sprint open-water event, which felt more like the real thing to me! Another first-timer option well worth considering is to enter as part of a relay team performing just one of the three legs. That way, you get to focus on your strongest discipline while experiencing the excitement of a race and getting firsthand insight into how it all works.

Where and when?

Think about when you want to race. The event's date will obviously dictate how long you have to get race-ready (and is particularly important if you are following a structured program, like the ones in Chapter Seven). The time of year will also influence the weather, which can have a big effect on how tough a race is. There are no guarantees that just because it's summer it will be warm and sunny or that early-season events will be tempered by rain and wind, but you can safely assume that water temperature will be higher later in the season. The size of the race is another important consideration for newbies. A huge event like the London Triathlon — the largest in the world — offers safety in numbers (you won't be last!), but smaller, local events can be a less daunting and more relaxed introduction to the sport.

You also need to take the race location into account. Are you prepared to travel a long distance? Most triathlons start very early in the morning and often you need to register the day before, so you may need to arrange overnight accommodation. If you are going to be far from home, will you mind not having friends and family around to

support you? (Or will they mind following you halfway across the country?!)

Horses for courses

The course itself is the next consideration. To make your first race experience as enjoyable as possible, I recommend finding out how challenging the leg of your weakest discipline is in any event that you're thinking about entering before you sign up. In other words, if you hate running hills, pick a race with a pancake-flat run leg to give yourself the best chance for a good experience. If you're nervous in open water, give events with choppy ocean swims a miss and look for placid lakes instead! On the following page are some of the key factors to think about regarding each leg.

The swim

- What type of start is it (see page 141)?
- Is it a mass start (where all competitors start together) or is the start divided into waves? (Waves are often divided by age.)
- How many people are there in each wave?
- How cold will the water be (partly dependent on the body of water, partly on the time of year)?
- How easy is it to navigate and sight?
- If it is a pool swim, what size is the pool?

The bike

- Is the route hilly? If so, how many hills and how steep?
- Are the roads closed to traffic?
- What is the road surface like?
- How technical is the course (in terms of sharp bends, steep inclines and declines and narrow sections, for example)?
- Is it a multi-lap course? You'll have to keep track of how many laps you've done.

The run

- Is the course hilly or flat?
- What is underfoot? Uneven, off-road terrain is much harder to navigate when you're fatigued — and you'll need to factor that in to your training.
- Will spectators be able to see you? This is when you need them most!
- Is the distance exact? If you hate running, the last thing you want is an extra half mile.
- Bear in mind that if you're taking on a sprint distance race or shorter, not too much can go wrong — if worst comes to worst, almost anyone can walk 3.1 miles (5 km)!

Race resources

Now that you've got some ideas about selecting the right event, how do you find out about races? The best starting point is the Internet. The official governing body of the sport in North America, USA Triathlon, has a comprehensive event listing on its Web site, as does the Australian Triathlon Association and you'll also find event information on commercial sites, like Tri247 and TriTalk (see Resources, page 172). These have the advantage of forums, where you can ask for advice and get feedback about races from other triathletes. Alternatively, do a local search to see what's nearby. Triathlon magazines, such as *Triathlon Life* and *Triathlete* also include a race directory, along with race reports that give you an insight into what different events are like.

Once you've earmarked a few possibilities, check out the event's own Web site, where you'll find entry details along with course maps, information about registration and so on — all of which should help you decide if this is the race for you. Once you've made your decision — enter! Races tend to fill up very quickly (particularly the big events) and the longer you have to prepare the better. Committing yourself to a concrete goal also boosts motivation.

Knowledge is power

Once you've entered a race, you will receive an information pack (some more detailed than others) by mail or e-mail. Make sure you read it in good time. It's no use realizing

---

SEVEN OTHER FACTORS TO CONSIDER BEFORE YOU FILL IN THE ENTRY FORM

1. When do you register and rack your bike? If it's the day before, you may need to fork out for overnight accommodation as well as race fees.
2. What are the accommodation options? Bear in mind that if it's a big city venue, hotels may be expensive. If it's a remote venue and a big race, accommodation will get booked up very quickly.
3. Is the race spectator-friendly? You'll be glad of the support of your friends and family cheering you on.
4. What are the logistics like? Is it easy to get to and park? Is it a race in which you'll finish at a different point from which you started? If so, how will you get back?
5. How far is the race venue from home? You are unlikely to perform at your best if you've just sat in a car for six hours or got off a long flight. Remember also that you may have to drive home tired after what is often a crack-of-dawn start.
6. What is the general standard of the race? There are races that always attract an experienced, fast field (such as those that double up as championship races) and others that are less competitive and more beginner-friendly.
7. Are the distances exact? If you're looking to see how you've improved, it's frustrating to find that the "Olympic" distance race you did was actually a 23.6 mile (38 km) bike ride and a 6.7 mile (10.9 km) run.

you were supposed to register for the race the day before when it *is* the day before and you are nowhere near the race venue! In fact, I'd advise taking notes when you read through the race pack and/or Web site. This arms you with all the information about your chosen race so you can get as prepared as possible before the big day. Pay special attention to the race rules, as these can vary a good deal from race to race.

Book your accommodation, sort out your travel arrangements and, if it's not too far away, go and look at the course. Could you make a training weekend of it? If you can't visit, study the course map so that you can factor in any relevant things to your training — for example, if it's a hilly bike course, there's little point only doing flat rides. You may also want to change or upgrade your equipment to suit the demands of the course. For example, shoes with good traction for an off-road run or tinted goggles for a swim in bright sunshine.

Winding down

Whether you're following one of the programs in Chapter Seven or have planned your own regime, you should work back from the date of the race to the present to make the best use of your training time. But don't expect to train right up to the eleventh hour.

As race day approaches, you need to start reducing the volume of your training in order to maximize your recovery and feel fresh on

the day. This is called the taper — and you ignore it at your peril! Trying to train right up to the last moment before your race will hinder, not help, your performance. Even if you didn't manage to fulfill all you hoped to in training, trying to cram in last-minute training sessions isn't the way to go. So how do you taper properly?

Tapering your training

The key thing is to reduce the overall amount of training you do rather than the intensity or frequency. Research suggests that the reduction in training volume needs to be at least 50 percent compared to the previous week. For example, if you were doing a 60-minute easy run, that becomes a 30-minute easy run. The aim is to reduce quantity rather than quality, so you'd still include sessions such as tempo pace intervals, but just fewer of them. This prevents you from feeling sluggish. A study from the University of East Carolina found that an 8-day taper helped runners knock 29 seconds, on average, off their 3.1 mile (5 km) race time. The athletes reduced their training volume by 70 percent, but included some daily race pace intervals.

The length of the taper depends on how long and hard you've been training, how accustomed you are to regular exercise, and what distance the event is. Someone who has already done lots of races won't need as long as someone taking on their first race, for example.

In general, you need just a few days for a sprint distance event and maybe seven to ten days for an Olympic. The fitness gains from a good taper can produce a 3 percent improvement in race time. For a 2 hour 30 minute Olympic distance race, that would mean finishing 4.5 minutes faster.

But you can have too much of a good thing! An overly long or easy taper will not improve your performance. Tapering is a bit of a personal thing — and you'll learn from experience how long you need to perform at your best.

If you're intending to race practically every weekend throughout the triathlon season, then obviously you can't taper for all your races — you'll just have to make do with a couple of easier days either side of the event and focus your tapering on your most important races.

Eat wisely

Your training volume isn't the only thing that should be reduced during the taper. Given that you aren't expending so many calories, you also need to adjust your food allowance to reflect this. But don't overdo it — remember you've still got a big physical challenge ahead, so this is not the time to go on a diet! The key thing is to make sure your carbohydrate intake stays high to maximize glycogen storage in your muscles while cutting down on excess calories from sugary drinks, energy bars, snacks and high-fat foods. You may feel a little heavy during your

THE PERFECT SEVEN-DAY TAPER

Assuming you've been training regularly in the lead-up to the race, this is how the last week might work, in order to give you sufficient rest and recovery and leave you raring to go on race day!

7 days to go: Last day of normal training.

6 days to go: Complete rest/walking.

5 days to go: Short swim with some race pace efforts.

4 days to go: 50 percent time/distance of normal bike OR 30 percent of distance/time of normal run with a few race pace efforts in each.

3 days to go: Short swim with some race pace efforts.

2 days to go: Complete rest.

1 day to go: 10 minutes in each discipline with a few race pace efforts. If circumstances don't allow you to do all three, just do what you can.

Race Day!

taper, as your glycogen stores are full and each gram of carbohydrate holds 3 grams of water with it. Don't see this as a reason to a) go out on a 50-mile bike ride or b) go on a crash diet. It's quite normal to feel like this and it won't affect your racing. There's lots more advice on nutrition in Chapter Nine.

Mind games

Not all race preparation is physical. It's also important that you are mentally geared up to perform. Psychological skills training is part and parcel of being a pro triathlete, but there are some basics that we lesser mortals can learn and benefit from.

Visualization — or mental rehearsal — is a key skill worth mastering. Picture yourself in the race — swimming with a nice, steady stroke. Visualize every detail of your transition routine, picture yourself mounting the bike and riding off feeling strong. Research suggests that the most powerful visualization isn't just running a movie in your head, but actually feeling the experience, using all your senses — smell, hearing, taste, sight and touch. This makes it almost real as far as your subconscious mind is concerned.

Another powerful strategy in building confidence is to address your fears. Richard Allen believes that it's the fear of the unknown that makes us nervous.

"Think about what could go wrong, and what you'll do if it does," he advises. "You want to be sure that your whole race won't fall apart just because one thing goes awry. The key thing is to address the things you're most worried about and decide how you'll deal with them. Once you have a strategy in place for every eventuality, you'll feel less nervous."

See the "What If?" panels later in this chapter and you'll probably find you share the same fears as many triathletes. Try to stay positive and channel your nervous

energy into making sure you are 100 percent prepared and ready. Then you can tell yourself truthfully "I am as prepared as I can possibly be for this race." Even if you don't really believe you are, acting as if you are can be very powerful. This technique entails acting as you would if you felt or behaved the way you would like to. So as far as the race is concerned, you have to act as if you are confident. What would you be feeling now if you were full of confidence? What would you be saying and hearing? Act as if that is really how you feel and you'll be amazed how your subconscious mind responds.

Associated with this, you can interpret the messages you get from your body differently — so rather than thinking those butterflies in your stomach mean you're really terrified, think of them as a sign of excitement.

One final mental exercise is to decide on one aspect of the race that you'll enjoy: the excitement of competing, the thrill of cycling on closed roads or hearing your friends and family cheering you on, for example.

"Many first-timers — and even experienced triathletes — forget to actually enjoy the race experience while it's happening," says Richard Allen.

I can certainly attest to this. In my first races I was so intent on remembering what to do next I had a frown of concentration on my face throughout and only smiled after I'd crossed the finish line. Remember, this is meant to be fun!

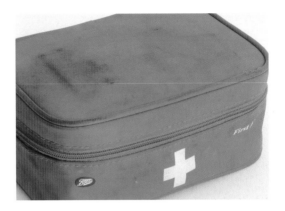

Practical preparation for race day

Given the amount of gear you need for a triathlon is about the same as you need for a week's holiday — it's worth making a list of everything you need in good time — from the big stuff, like a wetsuit and shoes, down to the little things, like your favorite energy gels, a race belt and some anti-chafing lube.

Your own personal list will be unique to you, but the checklist on the following page is a good starting point.

It's worth having your bike serviced 2–3 weeks before your race to allow time for any new adjustments or parts, like tires or cables, to settle and to make sure you're happy with the way it's riding post-service. Don't leave it until race week to book a bike service.

At many big races, there are on-site bike mechanics who will give your bike the once-over for a small fee. I frequently take up this offer, as I feel more confident when I know an expert has checked my bike — but it's not something the pros would do!

RACE DAY CHECKLIST

- Wetsuit (for open-water swims)
- Swimsuit/Tri suit (or whatever you will wear under your wetsuit for the rest of the race)
- Goggles — take two different pairs for different conditions, but never wear new ones on race day
- Swim cap
- Baby oil — to make wetsuit removal easier
- Lubricant (such as BodyGlide or Vaseline) — to prevent chafing, particularly around the neck area
- Towel — to help mark out your transition area and stand on to dry feet
- Bike
- Bike shoes (if you're wearing them)
- Elastic bands — to attach bike shoes to pedals, if you're doing this
- Helmet
- Sunglasses/eyewear
- Bike tool (for last-minute adjustments)
- Spare inner tube and gas cylinder or small pump (if you intend to repair an untimely puncture)
- Track pump
- Extra clothing (such as long-sleeved top and gloves, if it's too cold to cycle in just a tri suit)
- Plastic trash bag (to cover your gear in transition if it's raining)
- Running shoes (ideally with elastic laces for easy access)

- Socks — if you must!
- Hat or visor (optional — either to keep sun off or stay warm, depending on weather)
- Race information (including directions to the venue)
- Race numbers and/or race registration documents (you may need ID or your racing license)
- Timing chip (if you've been given one)
- Race belt (this saves you from pinning race numbers on your front and back)
- Water and energy drinks or gels and snacks (for before, during and after the race)
- Sunscreen
- Dry, warm clothing to put on post race.

Optionals:

- Rubber shoes (for walking around transition and wearing pre-race)
- Sports watch (many races use timing chips these days, but you might want to time yourself)
- A basic first-aid kit — a diarrhea drug, an analgesic, antiseptic wipes and blister Band-Aids
- A plastic crate to transport all your belongings — handy for post-race when your gear will be wet and dirty

Making race day a success

The big day is here. It's what you've been waiting for. This is when all your hard training should come to fruition. But to make sure that it does and that you don't foil your chances of success, this section will help you be as prepared as any Boy Scout could hope to be. Silly mistakes, like turning up without your favorite energy drink, trying to set off on your bike in a gear so high you can hardly turn the pedals or not being able to find it at all — they've all been done before and no doubt will be done again. But hopefully, not by you!

Getting there
It's almost impossible to get to the race too early. It isn't like a running event, where all you need to do is pick up your race number — you've got to register, set up your transition area and then work out where the swim starts and re-enters transition, where the bike exit and entrance are and where the run exit is. Then you'll want to warm up, get into your wetsuit and, if you're nervous, visit the bathroom half a dozen times! You may also need to attend a pre-race briefing — it's well worth going if there is one, as this will help allay your fears and doubts and inform you of any last-

minute course changes. Allow at least two hours for the whole process (unless you've registered and racked your bike the day before, as required by some larger events).

Registration

Registration simply involves picking up your race number, your timing chip (if the race issues them), swim cap, various stickers to attach to your bike and helmet and sometimes a wristband to allow you access to the transition area (which is not open to non-competitors). Some races also mark your lower leg and arm with your race number, which makes you feel like a real pro! For big events, allow time to line up for registration.

Once you've been through registration, there may be stalls or an expo to look around. Be wary about spending too much time on your feet and don't make the classic beginner's mistake of buying something brand new to wear for the race that you haven't had a chance to try out first.

Setting up

Once you've found or chosen your spot in transition, take a look around for a good landmark that will help you find it with ease. Is there something large, such as a sponsor's banner or a tree which you can use as a landmark? This may sound obvious, but don't use that brightly colored bike next to yours as a marker — the chances are it'll be gone by the time you get back to transition. How many rows along is your transition area from the swim entrance point? (I always take a permanent marker to write down the row and my race number down on my hand — it's amazing how disoriented you can feel when you emerge from the swim.)

Next, set up your transition area, as you've practiced in training (see page 86 for a reminder).

Take a look at the course

Start by checking out the swim course. How long will you need to allow to get there without a panic? What direction do you need to swim around the course and how many turn buoys will you need to navigate? Also be clear that you know how many laps you need to do, where you need to get out and the route back to transition. While you are taking yourself mentally through the swim, try to find non-moving objects, such as utility poles, cranes or trees that are in line with but higher than and beyond the buoys. Once you are at water level, it is much easier to spot a taller landmark, particularly when there's lots of splashing and other people around you.

Finally, look at the start line and decide where you'll position yourself along it. It's best to start wide and near the back, unless you are a strong, confident swimmer. The side you choose will be dictated by the position of the first buoy. If it is to the right, then you will need to position yourself to the left of the group and vice versa. Although this will entail swimming a few extra yards, it will allow you to avoid the worst of the chaos that is an inevitable part of open water swim starts. (Read more about race starts on page 141.)

Now it's time to walk from the swim entrance via your transition spot to the bike exit. And then from the bike entrance to the run exit, so you get your bearings for each leg of the race.

The final hour

Once you've completed your course reconnaissance and set up your transition area, double-check that you are ready for action with tires pumped, bike in an appropriate gear, pedals in the right position, drink bottles filled and mounted onto the bike and running shoes in place. There's little point in hanging around transition once you've mentally ticked off all these tasks, so find somewhere quiet where you can sit and chill out and go through your race plan. Depending on how long you've got, you may also want to eat or drink something in this final lead-up to the start.

Compact carbohydrates, such as sports gel, an energy bar or a muffin are a good way of boosting fuel intake in the couple of hours pre-race without leaving you feeling full. Research also suggests that caffeine taken an hour before exercise can improve performance in endurance events. This is something you should not risk on race day if you've not tried it in training — read more about how to use caffeine on page 158. This is also a good time to start sipping your sports drink of choice to make sure you start the swim well hydrated.

Suit up

When there are about 30 minutes to go, head back to transition to get your wetsuit on. This inevitably takes longer than you think it will — and it's really important to get it on properly (see page 98 for a reminder). If you have been given a timing chip, remember to put it on underneath the wetsuit. Once you're happy with the fit, apply some anti-chafing lubricant to the neck area and then zip up, making sure the zip cord is easily accessible.

If at all possible, flush your wetsuit through with water to seal it onto your body like a second skin. Do this by submerging yourself and pulling the neckline away to allow water to get inside the suit. Then squeeze the water out by pressing firmly along the front and back and arms and legs. You may get a chance to do this before the swim start.

Before you grab your swim cap and goggles, do a final check of your transition area. The aim is to walk away feeling confident that your transitions are as organized as they can be.

The swim

In open-water races, there are three types of starts. A deep water start (in which you are treading water until the whistle blows), a beach start (in which you run into the water) and a pontoon start (in which you dive or jump into the water). This latter type is rare outside elite events.

The advantage of a deep water start is that you get a chance to become accustomed to the water temperature and to swim a few warm-up strokes before the race. Once you've done that, get yourself into your chosen position.

When the gun is about to go off, try to lie fairly flat in the water to be in a position that is ready to swim, with one arm out in front, sculling to stay in position. (Sculling is moving the water in a horizontal figure eight pattern with your arms). When the gun goes, do one breaststroke kick to get your legs up and then begin to kick hard and turn your arms over quickly until the turmoil begins to subside and the group spreads out.

DIVING AND JUMPING

Not many open races entail a diving or jumping start, but some involve multiple laps, between which you have to get out of the water, run a short distance and then get back in — and this is where you may need to dive or jump. If you are diving, try to look at the very small area of water you will enter and make sure this point is a reasonable distance from the jetty — you want to dive forward, not down. Push off hard with the legs. Make yourself as streamlined as possible by putting one hand on top of the other, your arms beside your ears, dropping your head so that the crown hits the water first and not your goggles. If you jump in, hold your goggles in place to save time from messing around once you're in the water.

If your race involves a beach start, run as far into the water as possible, unless the surface makes it unsafe to do so. Lift and rotate your legs out to the sides rather than moving them straight up and down and drive with your arms. Wait until you naturally fall over and then use momentum to surge forward. You can start swimming at this stage or try "dolphining," if the water is shallow enough. Have your arms up beside your ears, as in a dive, and dive down toward the bottom. Grab the sand or rocks if you can and pull yourself along. Then spring up and repeat the movement. This gives you far better propulsion than swimming.

THE SWIM — WHAT IF...?

Someone knocks my goggles off
If you can retrieve them, tread water as you put them back on. It's worth the few seconds this will take to have good vision for the remainder of the swim. If they have disappeared, you have the option of swimming breaststroke with your head above the water if you don't want to submerge your eyes uncovered.
Prevention: Wear two swim caps — one over the top of your goggles strap — to help them stay in place.

I get a huge mouthful of water
Float on your back while you cough it out and wait till you can breathe properly before you resume swimming.
Prevention: Breathe to the side that is away from the direction of waves and chop (see Breathing skills, page 48).

Someone whacks me
If possible, just keep on swimming (you can get revenge later!). If you feel dizzy or in pain, float on your back for a moment to see if it passes. If you feel unable to continue, raise one arm in the air on your back, the signal that you need help.

My breathing clashes with my neighbor's
If you get someone's elbow in your face every time you breathe, try breathing to the other side or if you can't, swim to their other side.

I have a panic attack
Roll over onto your back and concentrate on your breathing. Your wetsuit will keep you afloat so you do not need to waste energy on treading water. Once you have calmed down, you can just roll over and try again. By this time, the crowds should have dispersed and you will have clear water in which to swim.

Stay on track

Once you're on your way, don't forget to sight. Following someone else isn't good enough — they may well be going the wrong way or swimming farther than is necessary — and remember your landmarks. If possible, get on to someone's feet and draft, which will also save you energy.

One of the most crowded places in an open-water swim is turning around the buoys. It can pay to swim wide rather than get involved in flailing arms and kicking legs. Shorten your stroke, particularly with the arm nearest the buoy and kick hard to enable you to make a tight turn. If the area is clear, you can swim close in to the buoy and perform a roll turn by flipping onto your back and corkscrewing, performing one backstroke with the arm closer to the buoy and then flipping back onto your front.

As you approach the finish, kick your legs a bit harder to redistribute blood flow from the upper body to the legs. Start thinking about what you've got to do next. You may feel unsteady on your feet when you get out of the water, so give yourself a few seconds to find your land legs before you head back to transition. Think about the location of your transition spot, remembering to use any landmarks you picked out during your reconnaissance or to count the appropriate number of rows. You should be removing your wetsuit as far as your hips as you run so you only have to pull it down and step out of it once you reach your bike. See Chapter Five for a reminder.

Pool know-how

A pool swim is less daunting than open water for most people, but there are still a few things worth knowing. Some races use a zig-zag pattern, in which you start in the far left lane of the pool, swim a lap and then gradually work your way across the pool to the far right lane. Others allocate swimmers to lanes according to their predicted speed. Whatever the scenario, be honest about your pace or you'll constantly be overtaken by other swimmers. If someone taps your feet during a length, you should wait at the next end for them to overtake you.

Try to find out what the swim protocol is before race day. It's also worth finding out whether the race allows flip turns, as some do not.

The bike

This is where all that transition practice comes into play. Chances are, if you've established a routine and practiced it enough, you'll find you are in and out of T1 faster than many of your competitors. Get yourself geared up for the bike and head for the bike exit — remembering not to get on until you have passed the mount line. No matter how relieved you are that the swim is out of the way, don't ride like a bat out of hell on the bike — you need to save some energy for the run. Keep your distance from other riders; drafting (riding in close proximity to the rider in front) is illegal in triathlon. If you are overtaking, you get 15 seconds to pass the rider in front. It's best to shout something out — "passing on your right/left," for example — particularly in beginner-friendly events where inexperienced cyclists might make sudden changes of speed or direction.

Remember to count your laps if it's a lap course. It's easy to get carried away and

THE BIKE — WHAT IF...?

I get a cramp

Cramps in the calves are common when you transition from swimming to cycling, as the foot position changes from the swim to the bike. If a cramp strikes, straighten your leg out and drop the heel lower than the toes, freewheeling. Massaging the sore area can also help.

Prevention: See page 171.

My drink bottle falls off

If you go to take a drink and inadvertently knock your bottle off the bike, it's a judgment call as to whether you should get it. If you've only just started the bike leg and only have one bottle, I would recommend retrieving it.

Prevention: Practice drinking on the move — and carry two bottles.

I can't get my feet in my shoes

If you opt for the elastic band technique of getting your shoes on while on the move but can't get them on, you have two options. Either be patient, riding along with your feet on the tops before trying again or stop, remove the shoes to put them on and then remount.

Prevention: Practice makes perfect. A little petroleum jelly on the back of the shoe can help your foot slide in easier.

I get a flat tire

If you get a flat during a sprint distance race or shorter, it's not worth trying to remedy it unless you are super-fast. In an Olympic distance race or longer, it may be worth replacing the inner tube — but obviously, you'll need to carry a spare, tire levers and a pump.

Prevention: Make sure your tires are not worn out (90 percent of punctures take place during the last 10 percent of a tire's life) before the race. Also make sure they are pumped up to their full recommended pressure, which reduces the risk of punctures.

forget. A bike computer can be handy here, as you can monitor your distance. As you approach the bike finish, spin your legs around in an easy gear to help flush out lactic acid and try standing up out of the saddle to stretch them in preparation for the run. Look out for the dismount line and make sure you're off your bike, using the method you've practiced in training, before you reach it. Be wary of people stopping right in front of you around the dismount line.

Wheel your bike back to your transition area and replace it on the bike rack before you take your helmet off. As mentioned in Chapter Five, it's best to rack your bike by the brake levers this time, to save having to turn it around. Change your shoes (unless you cycled in running shoes) and grab anything else you need for the run. Oh and don't forget, as I did once, to take off your bike helmet. It won't improve your run experience!

The run

There's no doubt that your legs are going to feel mighty funny for the first few hundred yards of the run. Expect it and it won't come as such a shock. The best approach is to set off taking small, rapid strides — keeping your upper body nice and relaxed. After a short while you'll get into your stride — and when you do, stay there. While you might feel you have a psychological advantage by flying out of transition as if you are about to perform a 400 meter sprint, the plan will backfire unless you are a very strong runner who can run well off the bike.

Research shows that even-paced running covers distance quicker than starting off fast and then slowing. So-called negative split running is when you run the first half of a race slower than the second — conserving energy in the early stages to utilize later. It is often used in marathon running to great effect, but we're talking a minute or two for a marathon — not 10 minutes — making the difference in a 3.1 mile (5 km) or 6.2 mile

THE RUN — WHAT IF...?

I run out of energy

Take it one step at a time. Don't think about the entire distance, just the next step. It's fine to walk if you need to.

Prevention: Make sure you take enough fluid and fuel on board during the bike leg. Consider carrying a sports drink with you on the run.

I feel nauseous or need the bathroom

The sudden jolting of the body through running after being supported on the bike and during the swim can churn up your insides. That's why it's so important to practice bike-run bricks in training.

Prevention: Sip, don't glug, fluid during the race. Make sure your sports drink or gel has no more than a 6–8 percent carbohydrate concentration. Higher levels can cause gastrointestinal distress. If you're worried about the runner's trots (diarrhea or loose stools induced by running) avoid high-fiber foods and caffeine on race morning and consider taking an anti-diarrhea drug.

I get a stitch

Stitches aren't exclusive to running, but do occur commonly as a result of it. Try putting your fingers into the painful area, breathing deeply, stretching out and coordinating your breathing with your footfalls. All of these work for some people, but none works for everyone!
Prevention: See page 170.

(10 km) just a matter of seconds. The greatest advantage of a negative split in triathlon is that it will prevent you from setting off too fast and spoiling your chances. Remember, it doesn't matter how impressive you were in the first kilometer — it's your pace as you approach the finish line that matters.

If you can hold a steady pace or run a slight negative split, you will almost certainly find you overtake people. Research shows that the majority of triathletes (outside of the elite races) slow down as the run leg progresses. There's much more joy to be had from overtaking people in the second half of the run than to be passed by droves of people you raced past at the start.

SEVEN TRIATHLON RULES — WRITTEN AND UNWRITTEN

Although official race rules vary from one association to another and even from race to race, heeding the following advice will stand you in good stead wherever you're competing.

1. Do not get anyone to assist you (other than a marshal) once the race has started.
2. Do not unclip — let alone take off — your helmet until your bike is racked and you are no longer touching it.
3. Your race number must be displayed on your back during the bike leg and on your front during the run.
4. Do not inadvertently draft behind another cyclist during the bike ride. You get 15 seconds to overtake.
5. Do not encroach on your neighbor's transition area and be considerate when you're discarding items in T1 and T2.
6. Remember not to get on your bike before the mount line and to get off it before the dismount line.
7. Be considerate when your race is over and you are leaving the transition area if other people are still racing.

CHAPTER NINE THE FUEL

No matter how fantastic your training regime is, if you don't fuel your efforts with the right type — and amount — of nutrition and hydration, you won't perform (or recover from) your training as well as you should. Good nutritional habits will ensure that you have sufficient energy to train, that you maintain a healthy body weight and body fat level, that your immune system is robust and that your body can repair the damage done by training.

The healthy training diet

What sort of diet puts a tick in all these boxes? Well, like any healthy diet, you need a balance and variety of nutrients — with plenty of whole grains, fresh vegetables and fruit, not too much fat or processed food and sufficient protein from fish, meat, eggs, dairy products or a range of nonanimal-derived sources. But there are two main differences between a normal healthy diet and one suited to an endurance athlete (yes, that's you!) — and they are energy intake and carbohydrate content.

As far as energy (or calorie) intake is concerned, you need to make sure you are eating enough to meet your energy expenditure. If you are regularly consuming less than you're expending, you'll eventually suffer from fatigue and poor performance, as well as greater susceptibility to illness and injury. Insufficient energy intake also has a detrimental effect on muscle mass and bone health. None of which is going to help you reach your triathlon goals! The formula on page 152 offers a guideline to calculating your energy needs. For a more detailed picture, consult a qualified sports dietician for a personal assessment and program (see Resources, page 172, for details). Incidentally, it's worth noting that additional carbs are the best way to fuel higher energy needs — but don't see this as carte blanche to stuff your face with pizza, cake and ice cream!

Carbing up

As for carbohydrates, well, these should be the star of the show in every meal and snack you eat. Carbohydrates are stored in the body (predominantly in the muscles and liver) in the form of glycogen — and this is the main energy source for physical activity. Even during low to moderate intensity exercise, carbs provide 50 percent of the energy required (the rest coming from fat) and that figure rises as exercise intensity increases. The reason you need to eat carbohydrates so regularly is that the body's capacity to store it is limited — and your training is constantly eating into those stores and depleting them.

Depending on how many hours training you do, you need a minimum of 6 grams per kg (2.2 pounds) of body weight each day — as much as 10 grams if you put in very long training hours, according to the latest

TRI TALK
Antioxidants Substances that combat the oxidizing effects of strenuous exercise and pollution.
Ergogenic Something that enhances performance.
Glycemic index (GI) A measure of how fast glucose is released into the bloodstream after consuming a carbohydrate.
Hyponatremia A condition in which there is too low a sodium concentration in the blood.
Isotonic A formula designed to rapidly replace fluid and salts lost from the body during exercise.
Macronutrients The major food groups required by the body, such as carbohydrates, protein and fat.
Resting metabolic rate (RMR) The rate at which you burn calories when you are at rest, to keep the body idling.

guidelines from the American College of Sports Medicine. So, for someone weighing in at 70 kg (154 pounds), that means a minimum intake of 420 grams of carbohydrate per day — the equivalent of the carb content of 15 bananas! I should stress that these amounts are of the carbohydrate content itself, not of the food containing carbohydrate. For example, a baked potato might weigh, say, 250 grams, but its carbohydrate content is only 55 grams.

Amount, then, is very important. But so is the type of carbohydrate that you eat. In terms of good health, many studies have shown that carbohydrate foods that are low to moderate on the glycemic index (GI) are preferable, because they don't mess with insulin levels as much.

The glycemic index is a measure of how fast a food releases sugar into the bloodstream. Low to intermediate GI foods release energy slowly to help you through the day without energy lows, but as a triathlete, you'll find that higher GI foods provide a quick energy boost before a long or tough session. They can also help top up energy levels without adding too much bulk if you're having trouble achieving your target carb intake and they make good post-race recovery foods.

As a general rule, opt for lower GI foods where possible, because they are healthier — but factor in some higher GI stuff, such as jam, honey and energy gels when you need the extra energy they provide and you need it quickly.

One final word on carbs — don't think that your options are limited to pasta and bread. Some healthy low-GI options include starchy vegetables like sweet potatoes and squash, as well as basmati rice, whole wheat pita bread, quinoa, oatmeal, boiled potatoes and tortilla wraps.

Pro protein

While the carbohydrate is the essential nutrient for training, protein is the nutrient that helps you repair and regenerate afterward. Protein is actually part of the structure of muscle tissue, which is why, with a higher level of muscle breakdown caused by triathlon training, you need a slightly higher intake than the average couch potato. This may be particularly important in the first few weeks of training: research shows an increased need for protein in newly active people, as the body hasn't yet become accustomed to conserving and recycling protein. The American College of Sports Medicine recommends 1.2–1.4 grams per kilogram (2.2 pounds) of body weight per day for active people, compared to 0.8 gram for sedentary folk.

Fish and white meat are often recommended as the best options, but top sports dietician Karen Reid recommends eating lean red meat a couple of times a week. "It's a good quality protein source and also high in iron — an essential mineral for endurance athletes," she says. Vegetarian triathletes need to make sure they get sufficient protein from dairy products, soy and tofu, along with beans and pulses, nuts and seeds. They should also include plenty of dark green leafy vegetables and other iron-rich foods, such as eggs, dried fruit and fortified cereals.

The fat facts

The final macronutrient we need is fat. But sadly, there isn't a recommended "grams per kilogram body weight" amount, as the majority of us eat plenty already! Fat contains 9 calories per gram, whereas carbohydrate and protein both contain approximately 4 calories per gram. Fat also requires less energy to be metabolized than either carbohydrate or protein, so is more likely to end up as a spare tire than to be utilized as an energy source.

In general, the best way of reducing your fat intake is to focus on cutting down on the unhealthier sources of fat in your diet, such as saturated and trans fats from processed and refined foods, high-fat snacks and fast food. That leaves a greater proportion of your dietary fat coming from more healthful mono-unsaturated and polyunsaturated sources (think olive oil, nuts and seeds, avocado and oily fish). You don't have to ban yourself outright from eating certain foods — just eat the higher fat foods more sparingly and choose healthier options elsewhere in your diet.

Good timing

While what you eat is important, when you eat it is also highly relevant. Training with an empty tank is a waste of effort — taking some calories and fluid on board beforehand will help you get more out of your training session. Want proof? In a study published in *Medicine and Science in Sport and Exercise*, athletes exercised moderately hard until they were exhausted. In one trial, they ate a 400-calorie breakfast three hours before cycling. In the second trial, they simply had dinner the night before. When they rode on empty, they biked for only 109 minutes, compared to 136 minutes with breakfast.

The same principle holds for daytime exercise. If you've been slaving away at your desk and will be going directly to training, boost energy levels with a high GI snack an hour beforehand, such as some gummy bears. Or, if you're watching your calorie intake, have a lower GI snack a couple of hours before you train, such as a banana with yogurt or whole-grain crackers and honey.

As for the old adage about burning more fat when exercising on an empty stomach, well, it's true, to a degree. The problem is that it's very stressful on the immune system and it forces the body to turn protein (the very fabric of your muscles) into readily usable carbohydrate.

Timing is also important post-training. After a long training session, make sure you have a snack (or meal, if appropriate) within 20–30 minutes. This should be predominantly carbohydrates with some protein (a ratio of 3:1 is ideal — basing your carb intake on 1 gram per kg (2.2 pounds) of your body weight). Studies have shown that this is the perfect window to allow maximum absorption of the carbohydrates — wait until you've showered and stretched and that window will have closed. Foods that are moderate to high on the glycemic index will work fastest. Antioxidants, to repair damage caused by exercise stress and pollution, and salt to replace lost body salts and stimulate thirst, make a great recovery package. My post-race snack pack includes skim milk, a bag of pretzels and some fruit.

Fluid thinking

I said there were two crucial differences between a normal healthy diet and a training-focused diet — but actually there are three. Fluid intake is the third. Research shows that the maintenance of fluid balance and carbohydrates supply are the two key ergogenic (performance enhancing) factors in a successful race.

Even at rest, the body needs approximately 1 milliliter of water for every calorie consumed. It doesn't all need to come from water or even from fluid — in fact, around a third of our daily fluid intake comes from solid

food. But given that, as a triathlete, your energy intake is likely to be higher than the average person's and that physical exercise itself increases the need to replace water (lost as a result of sweating to cool the body), you may want to reassess your fluid intake, both on a daily consumption basis and during races.

Starting a session dehydrated or becoming dehydrated during that session will inevitably have an impact on performance. As an illustration, a runner who normally covers 6.2 miles (10 km) in 35 minutes would slow by 84 seconds if he or she were dehydrated sufficiently to cause a 2 percent drop in body weight. Why does dehydration affect performance? Well, water makes up 93 percent of blood, whose job it is to transport oxygen and nutrients to the cells and remove carbon dioxide and metabolic waste. If blood volume is reduced through water loss, it becomes more viscous and the heart has to work harder to pump it around the body. Sweat rate is also reduced (to conserve precious water), increasing the risk of overheating.

How much to drink

The ideal, then, is to prevent detrimental fluid loss by starting sessions well hydrated, taking fluid on board on the move and making sure you rehydrate afterward. But what does that actually boil down to, in terms of how much you should be drinking?

Well, gone are the days when expert bodies such as the American College of Sports Medicine (ACSM) prescribed set volumes of fluid per hour for everyone. In 2007, the ACSM produced new guidelines on fluid intake for athletes recommending customized fluid replacement programs, owing to the huge range in sweat rates from individual to individual and the electrolyte content (especially sodium) of that sweat.

Not very helpfully, that means you need to work out what's uniquely appropriate for you (although the ACSM states that this is likely to be somewhere in the region of 13–27 ounces per hour of exercise).

But believe me, your fluid needs may not be anything like your training buddy's. I took part in a Gatorade Sweat Test, during which I had to ride an exercise bike for half an hour while my fluid loss was monitored. I lost 30 ounces in the 30-minute ride. My friend, on the bike next to me (in identical conditions) lost $3^{1}/_{2}$ ounces! That's why it's so important to get familiar with your own fluid needs by monitoring your intake and loss during training.

DEHYDRATION SYMPTOMS

- Fatigue
- Headache
- Poor performance
- Dizziness
- Lack of urination
- Muscle cramps
- Confusion

HOT TIP

To drink on the move, hold the bottle to the side of your mouth and tilt it upward, rather than hold it directly in front of you, which will entail having to tip your head right back. With the bottle to the side you should still be able to see where you're going.

One strategy is to weigh yourself naked before and after a training session (toweled down to remove excess sweat) of a measured time (30–60 minutes is ideal) without taking fluid on board. The amount of weight lost is water weight. Each gram lost equates to 1 milliliter of fluid, which gives you a guideline of how much you need to take on board in future sessions. It's not necessary to replace every single drop, however — studies show that replacing 80 percent of what you've lost is a realistic target. There are a few other factors to bear in mind:

- Weather conditions during your assessment. You'll sweat more in hotter weather.
- The type of activity. Fluid loss will vary between running, swimming and cycling.
- The intensity of the activity. You'll lose more sweat when you're working harder.

Another way of monitoring your hydration state is simply assessing your thirst. While expert opinion has long held that if you're thirsty, you're already dehydrated, more recent research suggests that thirst can be trusted. A study by researchers at the University of Cape Town found that cyclists who were forced to replace their actual total sweat loss in fluid intake performed worse than when they drank instinctively.

A third indicator of your hydration status (though one that is more useful post-training than during) is the color of your urine. Small volumes of dark-colored urine are a sign of dehydration — the ideal is to be producing normal amounts of light or straw-colored urine.

What to drink

Now you know how much to drink, what should be in that bottle? The main deciding factor is how long and how hard you'll be training. If it's a moderate session lasting under an hour, the research shows fairly conclusively that water is just fine. If, however, you're exercising for more than 90 minutes or particularly hard, a carbohydrate-electrolyte drink will give you more staying power. In fact, according to sports nutritionist Dan Benardot, finding a carbohydrate-electrolyte drink that you can stomach well and like is the single most important thing you can do to aid your performance nutritionally. The jury is still out on the 60–90 minute bracket, so experiment to see whether sports drinks or water works better for you.

An appropriate sports drink to take during training contains a 4–8 percent carbohydrate solution — this isotonic formula means that the fluid has the same gastric emptying rate as water, which means it helps to get the carbs it contains into the bloodstream quickly. It should also contain electrolytes (mainly sodium and potassium) to offset the losses of these substances through sweat. Another

important consideration is taste — research shows that an exerciser will drink more during a session if they like the flavor.

Too little, too much?

While dehydration is the main health issue as far as fluid intake is concerned, there has been a lot of recent media coverage of the opposite condition — drinking too much fluid. Hyponatremia, translated literally, means low sodium concentration in the blood. Exercise-associated hyponatremia is caused by overconsumption of water — usually a case of drinking too much, too quickly, so that the amount taken in exceeds the amount lost through sweat.

Nobody is immune to exercise-associated hyponatremia. But some people are more susceptible than others and some activities — including long-distance triathlons — are riskier than others. Research published in the *New England Journal of Medicine* on hyponatremia in marathon runners found that those with a low body mass index, a higher proportion of body fat to muscle or a small body size were at greater risk than larger athletes.

The symptoms of hyponatremia include muscle weakness, disorientation, swollen hands and feet, headache, nausea and breathing difficulties — and, in serious cases, the condition can cause

THE CAFFEINE FIX

While the jury is decidedly out on many so-called performance-enhancing substances, that isn't the case with caffeine. Research shows pretty conclusively that it improves endurance exercise performance. One study at the Australian Institute of Sport found that athletes who took a small quantity of caffeine could exercise up to 30 percent longer than those who took a placebo. Scientists believe this is mainly because caffeine reduces your perception of effort — as well as increasing alertness and concentration and possibly improving neuromuscular pathways. Start with a dose equal to 1 milligram per kg (2.2 pounds) of your body weight (equivalent to two cups of tea or coffee or one Red Bull) and see how you fare. You may need a higher dose if you are insensitive to caffeine if you use it a lot in daily life. (A report in the journal *Sports Medicine* states that doses of 6 milligrams per kg body weight is safe and ergogenic.) And remember, it doesn't have to be coffee — there are caffeine pills and energy gels containing equivalent amounts of caffeine. For optimal benefits, take caffeine 60–70 minutes before you train or race.

swelling, leading to collapse, coma or even death. Unfortunately, some of these are similar to the symptoms of dehydration (see box on page 156).

So how can you tell the difference and not make the grave mistake of mistaking hyponatremia for dehydration? It's best to think logically about your situation. Excessive drinking — whether it is before, during or after training dramatically raises the risk of hyponatremia, so it's important to monitor both your fluid intake and how you feel. Have you been drinking lots of fluids in the lead-up to the race and taking water on board often? If so, it's unlikely that you are dehydrated. If, on the other hand, you've been running at a fairly hard pace and have been sweating profusely, you may need to consider taking a little more fluid on board.

If you suspect hyponatremia in yourself or another athlete, it's essential to seek medical help immediately. The faster and lower blood sodium falls, the greater the risk, so the sooner the situation is assessed, the better.

Fueling up on the move

So that's the bigger picture, as far as nutrition is concerned. But what about fueling up during training and racing? The two key concerns are maintaining energy, through taking carbohydrates on board and topping up fluid levels. We've already looked at how to determine how much fluid you need — but what about the carbohydrates?

In a sprint distance race or shorter training session, carbohydrates aren't essential, as you won't be exercising long enough to deplete stores. But in longer races and sessions, it has been shown to increase endurance and performance.

You can get your carbs from a sports drink (see page 157), energy gels or, if you can stomach it, real food and energy bars. Gels are really just a concentrated form of sports drink, but you need to

remember to take plenty of water with them (follow the guidelines on the packet). Easily digestible food options include bananas (the riper, the higher the GI) and dried fruit.

Guidelines usually suggest that around 60 grams of carbohydrate per hour (the equivalent of 2-3 energy gels) is sufficient to offset glycogen loss during strenuous endurance exercise. You may want to go slightly higher than 60 grams per hour if you're taking on a half Ironman race or longer. Don't leave it longer than 30 minutes into your session to start taking these extra carbohydrates on board, as they takes time to be utilized.

Given that you won't have access to fluid (the lake or ocean aside!) during the swim leg, it is crucial that you begin drinking as soon as possible on the bike. In fact, being the longest leg of the race and the one in which it is easiest to drink and/or eat, the bike is the place to focus on your nutrition. Remember to practice eating and drinking on the move in training.

Food, drink and recovery

You might think that once your training session or race is over, you can stop thinking about what you eat and drink. Wrong! The right kind of nutrition can help aid your recovery, repair the damage done by training and enhance your fitness adaptations.

There are now designated recovery drinks and products, designed for ease of use and convenience, but milk-based drinks have also been shown to be effective, as they

VOICE OF EXPERIENCE: RICHARD ALLEN

Find out what sports drinks, if any, are available on the course during race day so that you can experiment with them in training to see if they work for you. Remember to take your own drinks, gels and foodstuffs to the race and, in the final 24 hours, don't drink or eat anything that you haven't tried before.

contain a good balance of high-quality protein and carbs. A study at Northumbria University compared the effects of a traditional carbohydrate sports drink with water and a milk-based drink on recovery from one exercise session and performance in a subsequent one. The cyclists taking the milk drink performed the best in the second exercise bout, indicating that they had recovered more successfully than the other two groups.

Sports nutritionist Karen Reid breaks the recovery process down into three phases: rehydration, replenishment and repair. "In dietary terms, that means you need fluid and electrolytes, the right amount of easily-absorbed carbohydrate and a good quality source of protein," she explains. "You have to get these steps in the right order, because if the cells are dehydrated, you can't transport nutrients to them — nor can you synthesize glycogen, as each gram is stored with 3 grams of water. Hydration has to come first."

But what's the best option? Well, a sports drink will provide fluid, electrolytes and some carbohydrates, so it's a good all-rounder. But if you've been guzzling sports drinks on the bike all day, you may find that the last thing you want is something else sugary, in which case, water, along with a salty snack, is a good option.

Step two is replenishment, primarily of depleted glycogen (carbohydrate) stores. "A sandwich with a protein-based savory filling or a milkshake, along with a piece of fruit, helps to provide carbohydrates, protein, calories and some antioxidants to help deal with the oxidative stress placed on the body." Aim to consume 1 gram of carbohydrates per kg (2.2 pounds) of body weight, along with some protein — and do it as soon as possible. While 20–30 minutes after training is the optimal time to refuel, Reid says that there isn't so much urgency if you aren't going to be performing another session that day or the following morning — though you should still aim to eat within a couple of hours of training.

Repair is the final stage of the nutrition strategy. It's very common to do a tough session and then come down with a nasty bug a couple of days after because the immune system is simply too tired to combat it. However, research shows that taking protein along with your carbohydrates post-exercise can help attenuate this, as well as stimulate muscle repair. "[Fish with omega-3 oils] is really good for damping down inflammation and muscle soreness," says Reid. Your armory against infection should also include plenty of fresh fruit and vegetables.

Whether you opt for commercial recovery products or real food, the ultimate goal of recovery nutrition, according to Reid, is to ensure that you go to bed with everything in equilibrium — it's during sleep that the body repairs itself.

SEVEN RACE DAY NUTRITION TIPS

1. **Don't try to race on an empty tank, no matter how nervous you are. You need to top up energy levels by taking in some calories in the morning — even if it's a liquid meal replacement drink.**
2. **Do stick to familiar foods that you have tried and tested in training. Take food out of wrappers for easier access.**
3. **Don't overeat through nervousness or boredom before the race.**
4. **Do leave the nozzle of your drink bottle open to save having to fiddle with it when you grab it for a drink. Stick to eating and drinking on the flat and straight parts of the course, not on tricky bends or when climbing or descending steep slopes.**
5. **Don't glug down a lot of fluid at once. Frequent sipping is the best strategy.**
6. **Don't guzzle down energy bars and gels on the bike if you're doing a sprint distance race — you won't need them. A sports drink will suffice.**
7. **Don't forget to replenish fluids and carbohydrates after the race. Consuming a sports drink and foods containing sodium helps to promote rapid and complete rehydration, according to the Gatorade Sports Science Institute.**

CHAPTER TEN DAMAGE LIMITATION

With three sports to contend with, you might think that triathlon equals three times the injury risk of individual sports — but luckily that isn't the case, at least not as far as chronic injuries are concerned. Unlike a single sport, the variety in training means you're not repeating the same workouts day after day.

That's not to say that triathletes — especially those with poor technique or who train excessively — are immune to injury. (Research in the *International Journal of Sports Medicine* found that the number of weekly training hours was a predictive factor.) But abiding by some general rules should help you stay out of the sports injury clinic.

First of all, do not increase the volume of your training by too much too quickly. (See Chapter Seven for more information on putting a sensible, progressive program together.) How much is too much is a personal thing, but it's essential to make sure you incorporate sufficient rest into your training program. In particular, try to make your running days nonconsecutive — running is the activity most associated with injuries. That's why you should also avoid running on hard surfaces all the time. Running on trails or grass is much kinder to your joints and offers more variety underfoot. This improves lower leg strength and, mile for mile, presents a greater challenge to the body.

Whatever the session, do not neglect warming up and cooling down, and maintain your flexibility through regular mobilization and stretching. You might also consider regular sports massage — this can help you to avoid injury by alerting you to specific areas of tightness or soreness, which may later turn into more serious problems. It also helps to stretch out muscles and assists the recovery process.

Listen to your body — and respect its needs. Never continue training when you are so fatigued that you have lost your technique. Don't just ignore pains, aches and nagging problems and hope they will go away. If the problem doesn't respond to rest, ice and anti-inflammatories, see a sports medicine expert for a proper assessment and diagnosis.

Finally, use the right equipment — from running shoes to swim paddles and bike tires — and check your gear regularly to make sure it is in good working order and isn't worn out. Read more about selecting triathlon gear in Chapter Six.

A core issue

There's one other aspect of injury prevention worth considering — strength training —

TRI TALK

Acute injury One that occurs suddenly and without warning.

Chronic injury One caused by overuse or misuse of the body.

Core muscles The deep muscles present throughout the body that stabilize the skeletal system and support joints involved in a movement.

Exercise ball A large, inflatable ball used as an aid to exercise.

Phasic muscles The muscles that work to facilitate movement.

Resistance band A large elastic band used to perform exercises that target specific muscle groups.

and in particular, core strength training. While the core muscles are often identified as the muscles of the abdominal region, there are actually core muscles throughout the body, whose role it is to stabilize the joints involved in a movement while other muscles (called phasic muscles) facilitate that movement. For example, the deep abdominal muscles contract to protect the spine when you bend down to pick up a weight from the floor; the rotator cuff muscles stabilize the shoulder when you throw a ball, the gluteus medius stabilizes the pelvis when you move onto one leg. At least, that's what all these muscles *should* do. . . But in some cases, they become weak and dysfunctional and don't do their job properly, allowing other stronger muscles to take over. When these other muscles work overtime they can grow short and tight, causing imbalances throughout the body and raising the risk of injury.

That's the theory, anyway. The question that remains is whether specific core exercises are needed. One recent study in the *Journal of Strength and Conditioning Research* found that general strength exercises, such as dead lifts and squats, engaged these muscles as much as getting on the floor and focusing on them with specific core workouts did. But would that be the case if your core was not functioning properly?

While the research on core training and its effect on injury prevention and performance is mixed, most elite athletes now include core stability work in their training regimes. For the record, one study found that core training improved core stability but that this had no effect on running performance, while another study found that good core stability helped protect against and remedy iliotibial-band syndrome, a common running injury.

Personally, I've found core training immensely helpful in staying injury-free for the last eight years.

Basic core workout

If you feel you could benefit from adding some strength training to your program, see how you fare with this workout. Then, when you're comfortable with it, introduce some more functional strength work (by functional, I mean exercises that are more akin to the actual activities you do during your sport), such as squats, lunges, dead lifts, lat pulldowns, push-ups and dips. Make sure that you focus on good posture and technique throughout.

1

1. Kneeling extension
Works the deep abdominals and back.

Kneel with your hands below your shoulders and knees below hips, spine in neutral. Extend one arm and the opposite leg until they are parallel with the floor and hold for 5 seconds. Lower and raise the opposite limbs. Do three sets of eight extensions.

2a

2b

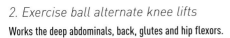

2. Exercise ball alternate knee lifts
Works the deep abdominals, back, glutes and hip flexors.

a. Lie back on a exercise ball until it is resting under your shoulder-blades. Take your arms out to the sides for balance and raise your hips until your torso is parallel to the floor.

b. Now lift one knee about 45 degrees off the floor, pause, then lower. Raise the opposite knee. Do three to four sets of eight lifts.

3a

3. Bridge
Works the lower back and glutes for pelvic stability.

a. Lie on the floor with knees bent and feet flat. Raise the body up enough to allow the pelvis to clear the floor. Hold for 10 seconds, then release. Do five repetitions.

3b

b. Once you can do this comfortably, raise your pelvis and then alternately extend one leg and then the other, without allowing the pelvis to tilt from side to side. Do three sets of eight.

4

4. Plank

Works the deep abdominals. A great exercise for cyclists.

Lie facedown, hands linked into a fist in front of your chest. Raise yourself up onto forearms and toes, keeping the back in a straight line and the tummy lifted. Keep shoulders drawn away from ears and retracted. Breathe freely and hold the position for 10 seconds. Rest and repeat twice more. Build up to 30-second holds.

5

5. Back and shoulder squeeze

Works the upper back and shoulder stabilizers.

Lie on your tummy, forehead resting on the floor and arms out to the sides, bent in a right angle. Draw your arms off the floor by squeezing the shoulder blades back and down — trying to keep the hands and elbows level. Hold for 5 seconds, lower and repeat. Once this gets easy, try holding light weights. Do three sets of eight.

6a

6. Hamstring curl on ball

Works the pelvic stabilizers, lower back and hamstrings. Great for runners.

a. Lie faceup with your heels on a Swiss ball, legs straight and arms by your sides.

b. Lift yourself up so that your body forms a straight line from head to heels and then, bending your knees, roll the ball in toward your bottom.

6b

Pause, then slowly roll it away again. Do three sets of eight. Progress to rolling the ball in with one leg at a time.

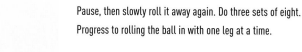

7a

7b

7c

7d

7. Shoulder rotation

Works the rotator cuff, a small group of postural muscles that stabilize the shoulder joint. Great for swimmers.

a. Hook a resistance band around the handle of a closed door or something else sturdy of a similar height. Take a few steps away so that the band is stretched and position your arm so that the upper arm is close to your side and the forearm at a right angle across your body.

b. Pulling against the resistance, hinge the arm open to the side, keeping the upper arm close to the torso. Pause, then return to the start position and repeat.

c. & d. Now turn around so that the resistance is coming from the other way (so that your arm is in the open position at the start and the resistance comes when you bring it across the body).

Do two sets of eight in each direction.

ICE PACKS
Apply crushed ice (which can mold well around the shape of a limb), frozen peas or a gel ice pack to the injured area for 8–12 minutes, then remove. Repeat every couple of hours. It isn't beneficial to use ice for longer than this. For a very specific point of pain, you can use ice massage. Try freezing a full paper or plastic cup of water and using its surface for massage.

Dealing with chronic injuries

Chronic injuries come in a whole range of guises — none of which responds well to denial! Signs of a chronic injury in muscle include tightness (sometimes in the form of a palpable knot or band of thickened tissue), pain or tenderness, and occasionally weakness. Around a joint, you'll expect swelling, pain and a reduced range of motion. You may find that as you get into your training session, these sensations wear off — but that doesn't mean the problem has gone. If it comes back later, you must address it to prevent it from getting worse.

The first thing to do is rest the injured area. Ice helps with most chronic injuries, as it reduces inflammation. Compression and elevation are more useful in the event of acute injuries (see opposite).

With chronic back problems, it's best to go on instinct as to whether to use ice or heat — if all the back muscles go into spasm, heat can help mobilize the area, while ice will just cause it to seize up further.

Resting an injured area doesn't mean keeping it completely immobile. In fact, it's important to gently stretch a muscle or take a joint through its full range of motion. But only do this if it doesn't cause further pain. For muscles, a little massage can help — use a nonsteroidal anti-inflammatory gel or try arnica balm — a homeopathic remedy favored by many physiotherapists.

After a couple of days, try some gentle activity. If you can do that pain-free, then gradually increase your training — taking care to maintain both your strength and flexibility in the surrounding area. If even gentle activity brings the problem on again, it's time to see a sports medicine expert.

Acute problems

Triathletes may get fewer chronic injuries than many single-sport athletes, but the bad news is that acute injuries — those that occur without warning — are more common. These tend to result from collisions or falls from the bike and can range from cuts and bruises to broken bones.

Road rash and bruising

Road rash is the euphemistic term for the cuts and abrasions that result from coming off your bike and more than likely, sliding a few feet along the ground. The resulting friction causes layers of skin to rub off. There is often little or no bleeding, but that doesn't stop road rash from being incredibly painful, due to nerve endings under the skin being exposed.

A serious case of road rash should be cleaned and dressed by a medical professional, but you can deal with less severe incidents yourself. Clean the wound thoroughly, removing any debris (ouch!) either through pouring water or saline solution onto the area to rinse it away or dabbing gently with a gauze pad. Don't use hydrogen peroxide to clean the wound, as this dries up the skin too much. It's now believed that keeping a wound moist better promotes healing and tissue formation.

Check for any deeper cuts while cleaning the damaged area. A cut that continues to bleed after 15 minutes or doesn't meet due to missing skin may need stitches. If you aren't sure, see a doctor or visit the emergency room, just in case. Once the wound is clean, cover the area with a breathable dressing, which you should change every few days. It's wise to keep your tetanus vaccine up to date.

If your bike crash doesn't break the skin, you'll probably end up black and blue at the point of impact. Bruising is caused by ruptured blood vessels leaking blood under the skin. A compression bandage can help, as can regular treatment with ice. If the bruising is midmuscle, stretching that muscle can also help, by tightening the fascia — soft connective tissue — around

VOICE OF EXPERIENCE: RICHARD ALLEN

You can often find clues to the causes of injuries by reviewing your training. Did you increase your training volume too quickly? When were you first aware of the injury as even the faintest nagging sensation? Are your shoes worn out? Have you still not got around to having your bike set up properly? Should you have rested after a hard race instead of pushing on with training? Look for any possible causes of the problem and address them. Always seek proper medical advice and rehabilitate injuries properly — otherwise you run the risk of re-injuring the same area.

the muscle, dissipating the collected blood. Arnica, a homeopathic anti-inflammatory, is also good for bruises.

Musculoskeletal injuries

Whether you break your collarbone, rupture your Achilles tendon, dislocate your shoulder or tear your hamstring, your first action should be to immobilize the area and take any weight or pressure off it. Then apply ice, or even cold water if you don't have ice. Never apply heat to an acute injury.

Compression and elevation of the injured part can also help, but don't take anti-inflammatory painkillers during the first 48 hours, as recent research has shown that this can interfere with the body's own healing mechanism. Ease the pain with an analgesic and steer clear of massage.

After 48 hours, you need to start to move the injured area through gentle stretching and mobility work. It's best to see a physiotherapist for a rehabilitation program — many athletes suffer from recurring injuries because they don't rehabilitate properly in the first place.

Other annoying problems

Ah, how we triathletes suffer for our sport. Here are a few of the more common ailments and what to do about them.

Blisters

Putting bike or running shoes on without socks might save time in transition but it can leave your feet covered in blisters. A blister is a buildup of fluid between the upper and lower layers of the skin, caused by repeated rubbing in a certain place. The best preventative strategy is to apply anti-chafing lube to vulnerable areas (such as the heels, the edge of the toes and the instep) or, if you're really blister-prone, apply a second-skin type of blister bandage before you even get one. Also make sure that your triathlon footwear fits properly and doesn't slip around on your feet. (Some people don't use elastic laces on their running shoes because they don't hold the foot as firmly as conventional laces.)

If you get a blister, only pop it if it feels painful. Use a sterilized needle and dab with antiseptic lotion. Otherwise, apply a blister bandage for at least 48 hours to allow the fluid to disperse.

Stitches

Stitches, also known as exercise-related transient abdominal pain (ETAP), affect most of us at some time or other but the true cause is still unknown. It used to be thought that the jarring action of running was to blame, but the fact that cyclists and swimmers also suffer puts a damper on that theory. So what are the other theories? Some research suggests that a lack of oxygen supply to the diaphragm muscle (the dome-shaped muscle that sits below the lungs) is a likely cause, but the most recent research, from the University of Newcastle in Australia, suggests that stitches could be caused by irritation of the peritoneum, a double-layered membrane that surrounds the abdominal cavity. The outer layer, the parietal peritoneum, lies closest to the abdominal muscles and attaches to the abominal wall, while the inner layer, the visceral peritoneum, is wrapped around the internal organs. Between the two membranes is a fluid-filled space (the peritoneal cavity) that allows them to slide freely over each other. The theory is that the parietal peritoneum becomes irritated, either because the amount of fluid between the two membranes is reduced as a result of blood flow being directed to the working muscles, or due to a distended stomach pushing the inner surface against it.

So how do you avoid that pain in your side? One of the most important things is to avoid drinking large amounts of fluid at once, which will distend the stomach. For the same reason, avoid eating a full meal in the two hours before training; recent research found this significantly increased the incidence of stitches in runners.

What you drink is also important. In one study, researchers examined the effect of different fluids on the likelihood of getting a stitch — a proprietary sports drink orange juice, flavored water and no fluid. The fruit juice was least well tolerated, increasing the incidence of stitches and bloating.

If you do get a stitch while running, you may find that coordinating your breathing with your footfalls helps to get rid of it.

Muscle cramps

Annoyingly, the cramp is another condition that scientists still don't have a concrete explanation for. It occurs most often in muscles that cross more than one joint, such as the gastrocnemius muscle in the calf, which crosses the ankle and knee, and it tends to happen when we are transitioning from one activity to another, even if one of those activities is sitting, driving or walking. That's one of the reasons it's so important to warm up before you begin training. Some experts believe that bad posture or poor biomechanics contribute to muscle cramps, by overstimulating the Golgi tendon organs, receptors in tendons that monitor muscular tension. This triggers a relaxation response

> # HOT TIP
> **On long bike rides, try getting out of the saddle every now and again and stretching out the calves and hamstrings to avoid cramps.**

in the relevant muscle and a simultaneous contraction in the opposing muscle, resulting in a cramp.

Another theory relates to dehydration and, in particular, lack of electrolyte salts. In a study from the University of Alabama, cramp sufferers were able to exercise nearly twice as long before getting cramps when they drank fluid that contained electrolytes, compared to fluid that did not. A lack of glycogen (which forces the body to use protein as a fuel) may also be a factor, so make sure you maintain your carbohydrate intake, during and after training.

If cramp does strike, stretch the muscle(s) immediately and if necessary, top up your fluid and electrolyte levels with a sports drink. In the longer term, work on your flexibility and on correcting any muscle imbalances or poor biomechanics.

Chafing

Sore skin, rubbed raw by chafing, will take your eye off the ball in training or racing, but it's easily avoided. Apply a lubricant to any areas likely to chafe, such as the neckline when you are wearing a wetsuit, the nipples if you're wearing a top on bare skin and the inner thighs and groin for cycling.

RESOURCES

International Triathlon Union

The ITU is an international body dealing mainly with professional triathlon, such as the world championships and triathlon within the Olympic Games. Find news, results, and athlete profiles on its Web site. www.triathlon.org

Multisport

Multisport Canada hosts the HSBC Triathlon Series each year in Ontario and the website specializes in all triathlon related services. www.multisports.com

World Triathlon Corporation

This U.S.-based commercial body organizes the official Ironman race series that take place globally, including the mother of all triathlons, the Hawaii Ironman. WTC also owns the half Ironman race series known as 70.3. WTC races are not officially recognized by the ITU but are held in great regard by triathletes as a whole. www.ironman.com

USA Triathlon

The governing body for multisport (triathlon and duathlon) across the U.S. Membership is open to all, and currently stands at over 100,000. There's some useful beginner's information on the Web site on training and racing. www.usatriathlon.org

The British Triathlon Federation

This is the UK's governing body for triathlon. Becoming a member gives you insurance, reduced race entry fees, and access to restricted areas of the Web site, as well as a quarterly magazine. Find news, information on the rules of the sport, and details of coaches, the 300+ clubs across the UK, and registered races on the Web site, too. www.britishtriathlon.org

Triathlon Australia

The country's governing body for triathlon for everyone from the beginner to the elite athlete. There's information on membership, events, clubs and coaches, and links to individual state organisations on its website. www.triathlon.org.au

Trisport

Trisport Canada hosts the Subaru Triathlon Series each year in Ontario and the trisports website is an online store selling equipment, gear, apparel, and all of the hard to find necessities that every triathlete needs, including triathlon wetsuits, bike travel cases, aero race wheels, hydration systems, aerobars, triathlon-specific clothing, and much, much more. www.trisports.com

Women's Triathlon

Women's triathlon is an Ontario-based, non-profit volunteer organization of female athletes committed to providing a supportive event experience for all female triathletes, especially beginners in the sport. www.womenstriathlon.com

COACHING

USAT Certified Coach Are you an athlete looking for a coach or mentor who can help you achieve your fitness, training, and racing goals? Take your performance to the next level by contacting a USAT Certified Coach in your area. www.usatriathlon.org

Richard Allen offers online coaching, training days, and triathlon camps to triathletes of all abilities. For more information, visit www.richardallenfitness.com

SWIMMING
Swimfortri

Swimfortri offers swim stroke improvement and coaching for swimmers and triathletes of all levels, both on a one-to-one and group basis. Their sessions take place in open water, a variety of pools, and at their endless pool facility with four-way filming. They also run training camps. www.swimfortri.com

Art of Swimming

Steven Shaw's Alexander technique–inspired approach to swimming emphasizes technique that works in harmony with the body—and the water. Art of Swimming teachers, courses and vacations can be found on the Web site. www.artofswimming.com

SwimTrek

Swimtrek, the world's leading adventure swimming specialists, offer open water swimming holidays, improvers' trips, and long-distance training camps in the Carribean, Middle East, UK and Europe. www.swimtrek.com

Open-water swimming venues

Open water swimming made its Olympic debut in 2008 and so it's a great time to get involved and take advantage of the expanding competitive opportunities. Get all the information about regular swim clubs, upcoming meets and venues. www.usaswimming.org

CYCLING

Adventure Cycling America's largest recreational cycling association has developed the National Bicycle Route Network, encompassing more than 24,000 miles of road and mountain bike trails, which are depicted on high-quality route map. www.adventurecycling.org

Bike Fit Studies show that 96% of the population is misaligned in their fit to their bicycle. Paul Swift, an 8-time USA National Champion, is one of the 96% that is biomechanically misaligned. Paul designed and developed products to help him attain success in racing. After applying his products to testing in studies at Auburn University, and learning that his products provide a competitive and safety advantage, Paul decided to share his knowledge to help others to enjoy their cycling even more. www.bikefit.com

Bicycle Coach Hiring a good coach is one of the best ways to reach your cycling goals and this site makes it easy by offering an official list of USA-Cycling-certified coaches. It also provides some free tips and articles by these coaches to improve your bicycling. The coaches are organized by state to make it easy to narrow your search. Plus, their email addresses and web sites (as applicable) are available, too. www.bicyclecoach.com

RUNNING

Chi Running—a method that marries some of the principles of tai chi with a specific running technique. www.chirunning.com

Pose Running—Dr. Nicholas Romanov's take on running technique, favoring a forefoot strike. www.posetech.com

The Art of Running—Canadian coach Malcolm Balk's take on running, incorporating the Alexander Technique. www.theartofrunning.com

The Davis Lab at the University of Delaware is where Dr. Irene Davis bases her research into the biomechanics of running and injury prevention. Read about her work at www.udel.edu/PT/davis/Lab.htm

ONLINE RETAILERS

Nice2Tri is a new online retailer run by triathletes and specializing in triathlon. It offers running, swimming, cycling, and tri-specific clothing along with footwear, eyewear, compression clothing, nutritional products, and training plans. www.nice2tri.com

Wiggle is one of the UK's biggest online sports retailers—particularly strong on bike gear—with delivery worldwide. www.wiggle.co.uk

3-athlon is an online triathlon store for swim, bike and run gear. www.3-athlon.com

Tri UK has a huge superstore in Yeovil, Somerset—complete with endless pool for wetsuit trials—and claims to be the world's largest online triathlon specialist. www.triuk.com

Mailsports is a swimwear online retailer with swim tools and triathlon gear on sale. www.mailsports.co.uk

CLOTHING AND GEAR

Swimwear and wetsuits
Speedo www.speedousa.com
Aquasphere www.aquasphereswim.com
2XU www.2xu.com
Orca www.orca.com
BlueSeventy www.blueseventy.com
Sailfish www.sailfish-wetsuits.com
Enduro www.endurosport.com

Running shoes
Adidas www.adidas.com
ASICS www.asicsamerica.com
Brooks www.brooksrunning.com
Keen www.keenfootwear.com
Mizuno www.mizunousa.com
New Balance www.newbalance.com
Nike www.nike.com
Pearl Izumi www.pearlizumi.com
Puma www.puma.com
Reebok www.reebok.com
Saucony www.saucony.com

Sports bras
For sports bras, try **www.lessbounce.com** for a comprehensive range from brands including Sportsjock, Shock Absorber, Enell and Nike.

Bike wear
Sugoi www.sugoi.com
Pearl Izumi www.pearlizumi.com
Gore www.gorebikewear.com
Endura www.endurasport.com
Rapha www.rapha.cc

Bike shoes
Shimano bike.shimano.com
Northwave www.northwave.com
Scott www.scottusa.com

Tri suits
2XU www.2xu.com
Craft www.craft.se
Zoot www.zootsports.com

Compression gear
Skins www.skins.net
2XU www.2xu.com

Performance and monitoring
Garmin GPS systems, heart rate monitors, and cadence sensors www.garmin.com
Polar heart rate monitors www.polarusa.com

NUTRITION

The Gatorade Sport Science Institute conducts research into sports nutrition and performance. Its Web site is a comprehensive source of articles, tips, research, and tools in these areas and on their products. www.gssiweb.com

Performance Food is dietician and sports nutritionist Karen Reid's Web-based service for athletes and sports people, providing education and resources on nutrition to give optimal sports performance. One-to-one nutritional analysis and advice is also available. www.performancefood.co.uk

INJURY PREVENTION

American Physical Therapy Association
Find a qualified physiotherapist in your area by visiting www.apta.org

American Massage Therapy Association
This is the professional body representing sports massage practitioners, with a national register of qualified therapists. www.amtamassage.org

INDEX

Photographic credits

WP = Whole Picture Productions, EJ = Eddie Jacob

p2–3 (l–r) WP, Corbis RF/Alamy, Corbis Super RF/Alamy, 6 Marcelo Sayao/epa/Corbis, 8 EJ, 9 Action Photo, 10 WP, 12 Tim Tadder/ Corbis, 13 F1online digitale Bildagentur GmbH/Alamy, 14 WP, 16-21 EJ, page 23-30 WP, 31 EJ, 32 (SFT) SwimforTri/Keeley Bullock, 34-42 EJ, 43-45 WP, 46,47 EJ, 48, 49 WP, 50 OJO Images Ltd/Alamy, 51 S. Carmona/CORBIS, 52 WP, 53 EJ, 54 WP, 58, 60 EJ,61–64 WP, 65 Gabe Palmer/CORBIS, 66 Andrew McCandlish/Alamy, 67 EJ, 68 WP, 69 EJ, 70 WP, 73 Corbis Super RF/Alamy, 74-77 WP, 78 Corbis Super RF/Alamy, 79 Mike Finn-Kelcey/Reuters/Corbis, 81 EJ, 82 WP, 84 Corbis Super RF/Alamy, 85-97 WP, 98 EJ, 99-103 WP, 104 EJ, 105 WP, 106, 107 EJ, 108–111 WP, 112 Andrew McCandlish/Alamy, 114 WP, 115 EJ, 116-127 WP, 128 Robert Michael/ Corbis, 129 EJ, 130 Cody Duncan/Alamy, 134 Anna Blume/Alamy, 135 EJ, 137 Corbis Super RF/Alamy, 138 WP, 139 EJ, 140 London Marathon Press Office, 141 Robert Michael/Corbis, 142-145 WP, 147 EJ, 148 F1online digitale Bildagentur GmbH/Alamy, 149 Corbis RF/Alamy, 150–155 EJ, 156 WP, 157 EJ, 158 WP, 160 Image Source Pink/Alamy, 162 Bill Marsh Royalty Free/Alamy, 164–167 EJ, 168 Guy Hearn, 169, 176 EJ

Photo of Richard Allen by Clare Booth